Understanding Agriculture

New Directions for Education

D1245830

Committee on Agricultural Education
in Secondary Schools
Board on Agriculture
National Research Council

NATIONAL ACADEMY PRESS
Washington, D.C. 1988

National Academy Press • 2101 Constitution Avenue, NW • Washington, DC 20418

NOTICE: The project that is the subject of this report was approved by the Governing Board of the National Research Council, whose members are drawn from the councils of the National Academy of Sciences, the National Academy of Engineering, and the Institute of Medicine. The members of the committee responsible for the report were chosen for their special competences and with regard for appropriate balance.

This report has been reviewed by a group other than the authors according to procedures approved by a Report Review Committee consisting of members of the National Academy of Sciences, the National Academy of Engineering, and the Institute of Medicine.

The National Academy of Sciences is a private, nonprofit, self-perpetuating society of distinguished scholars engaged in scientific and engineering research, dedicated to the furtherance of science and technology and to their use for the general welfare. Upon authority of the charter granted to it by the Congress in 1863, the Academy has a mandate that requires it to advise the federal government on scientific and technical matters. Dr. Frank Press is president of the National Academy of Sciences.

The National Academy of Engineering was established in 1964, under the charter of the National Academy of Sciences, as a parallel organization of outstanding engineers. It is autonomous in its administration and in the selection of its members, sharing with the National Academy of Sciences the responsibility for advising the federal government. The National Academy of Engineering also sponsors engineering programs aimed at meeting national needs, encourages education and research, and recognizes the superior achievements of engineers. Dr. Robert M. White is president of the National Academy of Engineering.

The Institute of Medicine was established in 1970 by the National Academy of Sciences to secure the services of eminent members of appropriate professions in the examination of policy matters pertaining to the health of the public. The Institute acts under the responsibility given to the National Academy of Sciences by its congressional charter to be an adviser to the federal government and, upon its own initiative, to identify issues of medical care, research, and education. Dr. Samuel O. Thier is president of the Institute of Medicine.

The National Research Council was established in 1916 to associate the broad community of science and technology with the Academy's purposes of furthering knowledge and advising the federal government. Functioning in accordance with the general policies determined by the Academy, the Council has become the principal operating agency of both the National Academy of Sciences and the National Academy of Engineering in providing services to the government, the public, and the scientific and engineering communities. The Council is administered jointly by both Academies and the Institute of Medicine. Dr. Frank Press and Dr. Robert M. White are chairman and vice chairman, respectively, of the National Research Council.

This project was supported under grant No. 59-32U4-5-11 from the Agricultural Research Service of the U.S. Department of Agriculture and grant No. G008520005 from the Department of Education. It has received funding from the National Research Council Fund, a pool of private, discretionary, nonfederal funds consisting of contributions from a consortium of private foundations including the Carnegie Corporation of New York, the Charles E. Culpeper Foundation, the William and Flora Hewlett Foundation, the John D. and Catherine T. MacArthur Foundation, the Andrew W. Mellon Foundation, the Rockefeller Foundation, and the Alfred P. Sloan Foundation. Support was also received from the Merck Company Foundation and the Idaho Vocational Agricultural Teachers Association. Preparation of this report was partially supported by the W. K. Kellogg Foundation.

Library of Congress Cataloging-in-Publication Data
Understanding agriculture: new directions for education/Committee
  on Agricultural Education in Secondary Schools, Board on
  Agriculture, National Research Council,
      p.   cm.
   Bibliography: p.
   Includes index.
   ISBN 0-309-03936-3
   1. Agricultural education—United States.   2. Vocational
education—United States.   3. Education and state—United States.
4. Curriculm planning—United States.   I. National Research
Council (U.S).   Board on Agriculture.   Committee on Agricultural
Education in Secondary Schools.
S533.U47 1988
630'.7'1273—dc19   88-13126
                                                             CIP

Copyright© 1988 by the National Academy of Sciences

Printed in the United States of America

Committee on Agricultural Education in Secondary Schools

DANIEL G. ALDRICH, *Chairman*, University of California, Irvine
GRAHAM BOYD, North Carolina State University
DALE BUTCHER, Benton Central High School, Oxford, Indiana
ANNE CAMPBELL, Former Commissioner of Education, Nebraska
J. BURTON ELLER, National Cattlemen's Association
DONALD E. EVANS, Pennsylvania State University
WILLIAM P. FLATT, University of Georgia
DON LOESLIE, Minnesota Association of Wheat Growers
RUSSELL G. MAWBY, W. K. Kellogg Foundation
JOHN MOORE, University of California, Riverside
MONTY MULTANEN, State Department of Education, Oregon
JAMES V. RISSER, Stanford University
STUART A. ROSENFELD, Southern Growth Policies Board
ELLEN S. RUSSELL, University of Illinois
J. ROBERT WARMBROD, Ohio State University
RON WILSON, Farm Credit Services
DALE WOLF, Delaware Development Office

Staff

CHARLES M. BENBROOK, *Project Officer*

Board on Agriculture

Preface

In the 1980s, many forces have challenged American agriculture and education. These forces include demographics; urbanization; rapid gains in worldwide agricultural production capacity; domestic farm and trade policies; lifestyle changes; global competition in basic and high-technology industries; the explosion in knowledge caused by increasingly sophisticated computers, digital equipment, and biotechnological techniques; specialization within the professions; and public expectations about the role of schools, the food supply, and public institutions. A growing number of educators, farmers, and those in agribusinesses and public institutions recognize the need to adjust policies. Our educational system must meet these challenges.

This study on agricultural education in the secondary schools was initiated in 1985 because of concerns about the declining profitability and international competitiveness of American agriculture, as well as concerns about declining enrollments, instructional content, and quality in agricultural education programs.

The National Research Council established the Committee on Agricultural Education in Secondary Schools at the request of the U.S. Secretaries of Agriculture and Education to assess the contributions of instruction in agriculture to the maintenance and improvement of U.S. agricultural productivity and economic competitiveness here and abroad. The committee was asked to offer recommendations regarding:

- **goals for instruction in agriculture;**
- **the subject matter and skills that should be stressed in curricula for different groups of students; and**

• **policy changes needed at the local, state, and national levels to facilitate the new and revised agricultural education programs in secondary schools.**

Shortly after the committee began its work, the Congress expanded the scope of this study to include an assessment of the potential use of modern communications and computer-based technology in teaching agriculture programs at the secondary school level.

Throughout the study, the committee met seven times. Members of the committee held five hearings in various regions of the country, organized two conferences, attended a national Future Farmers of America (FFA) convention, and visited nine schools. The committee contacted numerous individuals and organizations to collect information and insights about agricultural education. Many officials and experts in the U.S. Departments of Education and Agriculture provided valuable data and insights. Although the committee focused primarily on activities at the secondary school level, it also gathered and assessed information on agricultural educational efforts at the elementary school level and in teacher education programs at the college level.

The committee received statements and materials from more than 300 representatives from agribusinesses, farm organizations, agricultural education groups, and parent and youth organizations; elementary, secondary and postsecondary educators and administrators; futurists; and state and national policy leaders. The committee gratefully acknowledges the contributions of these individuals and organizations.

The committee uses the terms "agriculture" and "agricultural system" interchangeably throughout the report. These terms are used broadly and encompass the production of agricultural commodities, including food, fiber, wood products, horticultural crops, and other plant and animal products. The terms also include the financing, processing, marketing, and distribution of agricultural products; farm production supply and service industries; health, nutrition, and food consumption; the use and conservation of land and water resources; development and maintenance of recreational resources; and related economic, sociological, political, environmental, and cultural characteristics of the food and fiber system. An understanding of basic concepts and knowledge spanning and uniting all of these subjects define the term "agricultural literacy" found in this report.

The report that follows focuses on the two major elements of agricultural education—agricultural literacy (education *about* agriculture) and vocational agriculture (education *in* agriculture). It consists of an executive summary, two additional chapters, and three appendixes. The executive summary sets forth the committee's principal findings, conclusions, and recommendations. Chapter 2 discusses educational programs about agriculture for all students at the secondary school level with the goal of producing agriculturally literate citizens. Chapter 3 examines vocational agriculture education programs and explores recommendations for change. The appendixes review the evolution of agricultural education.

Like agriculture itself, agricultural education is at a crossroads. The committee believes that a renewed commitment to and broadening of agricultural education will ensure the skills and knowledge essential to the future vitality of American agriculture.

DANIEL G. ALDRICH
Chairman

Contents

Understanding
Agriculture

1

Executive Summary
and Recommendations

The committee's vision of what agricultural education is and should become at the secondary level if a competitive agricultural industry is to survive in this country builds on the programs and approaches of the past, but goes beyond them in scope and content. The committee's findings point to two basic challenges: first, agricultural education must become more than vocational agriculture. Second, major revisions are needed within vocational agriculture. In working toward both goals, educators should borrow from the best current programs, while creating new ways to deliver to more students educational opportunities in the agricultural sciences, agribusiness, nutrition, and land resource stewardship.

AGRICULTURAL LITERACY

It is necessary to understand throughout this report the committee's definition of agricultural education, which extends beyond traditional vocational programs. Agriculture is too important a topic to be taught only to the relatively small percentage of students considering careers in agriculture and pursuing vocational agriculture studies. With this in mind, the committee developed the idea of "agricultural literacy"— the goal of education *about* agriculture. The committee envisions that an agriculturally literate person's understanding of the food and fiber system includes its history and current economic, social, and environmental significance to all Americans. This definition encompasses some knowledge of food and fiber production, processing, and domestic and international marketing. As a complement to instruction in other

1

academic subjects, it also includes enough knowledge of nutrition to make informed personal choices about diet and health.

Achieving the goal of agricultural literacy will produce informed citizens able to participate in establishing the policies that will support a competitive agricultural industry in this country and abroad.

PRINCIPAL FINDINGS

- **Agricultural education in U.S. high schools usually does not extend beyond the offering of a vocational agriculture program.**

Only a small percentage of students enroll in these programs. Consequently, most high school students have limited or no access to vocational agriculture or agricultural literacy programs. Minority students in urban schools have the least access to these programs.

PRINCIPAL CONCLUSIONS AND RECOMMENDATIONS

- **The focus of agricultural education must change**

This conclusion is a reflection of the reality within agriculture and of changes within society. Agricultural education is more than vocational agriculture.

- **Beginning in kindergarten and continuing through twelfth grade, all students should receive some systematic instruction about agriculture.**

Much of this instruction could be incorporated into existing courses rather than taught in separate courses.

VOCATIONAL AGRICULTURE

Vocational agriculture is education *in* agriculture. It has a long history in American education. Most programs consist of three parts: classroom and laboratory instruction, supervised occupational experiences (SOEs), and membership in the National FFA (Future Farmers of America) Organization. A broader definition of vocational agriculture is needed because technological and structural changes in agricultural industries have enlarged the scope and number of careers. In the committee's view, vocational agriculture should give students the skills needed to enter and advance in careers such as farm production; agribusiness management and marketing; agricultural research and engineering; food science, processing, and retailing; banking; education; landscape architecture; urban planning; and other fields.

Change within agriculture is an ongoing process that will affect agricultural businesses and institutions. They must adapt to continue serving agriculture. The institution of vocational agriculture is no exception.

Principal Findings

• **For many years, vocational agriculture programs have had a positive effect on tens of thousands of people: students, their families, and residents of local communities.**

Through vocational agriculture programs, students have learned practical skills, developed self-confidence, and acquired leadership abilities.

• **White males have mainly made up enrollment in vocational agriculture programs in the past and continue to do so.**

During the past decade, the enrollment of females has increased. Female enrollment has concentrated in a limited number of specialized vocational agriculture programs. Enrollment of minorities in vocational agriculture programs is disproportionately low.

• **Much of the focus and content of many vocational agriculture programs is outdated.**

Production agriculture—farming—still dominates most programs, although it no longer represents a major proportion of the jobs in the total agricultural industry. Traditional vocational agriculture programs and the students' organization, the FFA, are not meeting the broader needs for agricultural education generated by changes in the food and fiber industries and society as a whole. SOE programs often do not reflect the broad range of opportunities in today's agricultural industry.

• **Vocational agriculture programs are uneven in quality.**

Excellent programs need to be sustained and built upon. Some programs warrant in-depth study and replication as model programs. Those that do not meet educational needs should be upgraded, consolidated, or, as a last resort, phased out.

• **Vocational agriculture programs in secondary schools are currently conducted as part of the federal and state systems of vocational education.**

Restrictions on the use of federal and state funds for vocational education apply to vocational agriculture programs. The federal and state system of vocational education requires that instruction in agriculture in secondary schools be designed primarily, if not exclusively, for vocational purposes. These systems tend to preserve the status quo.

PRINCIPAL CONCLUSIONS AND RECOMMENDATIONS

• **The success of reform in vocational agriculture programs relies on innovative programmatic leadership at the state and national levels.**

Major leadership challenges include developing the curriculum, revising the focus and content of FFA programs and activities, evaluating programs, educating teachers, assuring adequate resources, and creating a more flexible and adaptive legislative and budgetary framework.

• **Major revisions are needed within vocational agriculture.**

The relevance and scope of the curriculum, SOEs, and the FFA must be broadened. Vocational agriculture programs must be upgraded to prepare students more effectively for the study of agriculture in postsecondary schools and colleges and for current and future career opportunities in agricultural sciences, agribusinesses, marketing, management, and food production and processing.

• **The quality of vocational agriculture programs must be enhanced, in some cases substantially.**

All programs—including those now clearly superior in terms of educational achievements—should be made more accessible and relevant. Realistic steps must be taken to identify weak programs and improve them, merge them with other programs, or, as a last resort, phase them out.

• **The establishment of specialized magnet high schools for the agricultural sciences in major urban and suburban areas should be encouraged.**

These high schools should offer the full range of academic courses in addition to courses in the agricultural sciences, nutrition, horticulture, natural resources and the environment, agribusiness marketing and management, and other related agricultural subjects.

- **Teachers should seek out and share high-quality computer software and instructional materials and media for agricultural management and planning and for instructional application.**   *2*

The use of high-technology instructional media aids student achievement by enhancing the instructional process.

- **As a goal, all students enrolled in vocational agriculture programs should participate in worthwhile SOEs.**   *3*

In addition to employment-related and entrepreneurial SOEs, students should acquire supervised experience in land laboratories, agricultural mechanics laboratories, greenhouses, nurseries, and other facilities provided by schools. The primary emphasis of supervised experiences in which students participate should be on learning, with appreciation for earning. Students should not be penalized in their program standing or FFA activities if a suitable high-quality SOE is sometimes unavailable, however.

- **The FFA should change its name and revise its symbols, rituals, contests, awards, and requirements for membership consistent with all applicable federal and state laws to reflect a contemporary image of agriculture and a broadened and improved agricultural education program.**   */*

EDUCATION ABOUT AND IN AGRICULTURE

Conclusions and Recommendations

The following conclusions and recommendations apply to agricultural literacy *and* vocational agriculture.

- **Programmatic and budgetary policy changes are needed at both state and federal levels if comprehensive programs of education in and about agriculture are to be implemented.**   */*

The comprehensive program of education in and about agriculture that the committee recommends will be impossible to bring about if the program is undertaken solely within the *existing* policies of the federal and state system of vocational education. The committee does not expect that agricultural literacy initiatives, including programs to foster career exploration and teaching science through agriculture, will emerge solely from the vocational segment of agricultural education. If they do, their acceptability to students and school system leaders is likely to be limited.

Financial support and technical resources must be directed toward new initiatives if progress is to be made in achieving agricultural literacy goals or reforming vocational agriculture programs. The committee emphasizes that it does not advocate or see the need for the redirection of funds from viable vocational agriculture programs to the support of agricultural literacy efforts. The redirection of funds may be permitted from vocational agriculture programs that are undersubscribed, however. Agricultural literacy initiatives warrant public support as a part of the educational reform movement agenda.

- **States should establish commissions, preferably appointed by the governor and the chief state school officer, to identify needs and strategies for implementing agricultural literacy programs and reforming vocational agriculture programs.**
- **Not only teachers and other specialists in agricultural education, but also legislators, school superintendents and board members, principals, and science teachers should provide leadership in the initiation of agricultural literacy efforts and the reformation of vocational agriculture.**

State departments of education and officials in leadership positions should acknowledge that leadership for all agricultural education programs need not be under the aegis of vocational agriculture.

- **The subject matter of instruction about agriculture and instruction in agriculture must be broadened.**

The dominance of production agriculture in the curriculum must give way to a much broader agenda, including the utilization of agricultural commodities, agribusiness marketing and management in a global economy, public policy, environmental and resource management, nutrition, and health.

- **Exemplary programs in local schools that have broadened the curriculum and improved the attractiveness of agricultural education programs should be identified, studied, and emulated.**

State departments of education, the U.S. Departments of Agriculture and Education, national professional organizations in agricultural education, and the National Council for Vocational and Technical Education in Agriculture should take leading roles in compiling and disseminating information about successful efforts to develop new programs and strengthen existing ones.

- **Teacher preparation and in-service education programs must be revised and expanded to develop more competent teach-**

ers and other professional personnel to staff, administer, and supervise educational programs in and about agriculture.

Colleges of agriculture, particularly in land-grant universities, should become more involved in teacher preparation and in-service education programs, curriculum reform, and the development of instructional materials and media. The committee recommends that land-grant universities establish a center for curriculum design and personnel development to accomplish these purposes. The committee further recommends that the U.S. Department of Agriculture encourage the achievement of this goal by providing challenge grants to universities initiating new linkages between departments in colleges of agriculture and agricultural education in the public schools.

2

Agricultural Literacy

Agriculture—broadly defined—is too important a topic to be taught only to the relatively small percentage of students considering careers in agriculture and pursuing vocational agriculture studies.

Students should come to appreciate that the species providing our food and fiber are part of a vast web of life that functions as an integrated whole. Every species of plant and animal depends not only on its physical environment but on the biological component of the environment as well. All living creatures are part of the same cycles of matter and energy. Thus, education will be incomplete unless students learn what is essential for the lives of our crops, animals, and plants. (Moore, 1987)

Agriculture encompasses the study of economics, technology, politics, sociology, international relations and trade, and environmental problems, in addition to biology (Moore, 1987).

The committee concluded that at least some instruction about agriculture should be offered to all students, regardless of their career goals or whether they are urban, suburban, or rural. With this in mind, the committee developed the idea of "agricultural literacy"—the goal of education about agriculture. Education in agriculture refers to the vocational component of agricultural education. This component is currently implemented at several levels—secondary, community college, university, and nondegree adult education programs in agriculture.

The committee envisions that an agriculturally literate person's understanding of the food and fiber system would include its history and its current economic, social, and environmental significance to all

8

Americans. This definition is purposely broad, and encompasses some knowledge of food and fiber production, processing, and domestic and international marketing. As a complement to instruction in other academic subjects, it also includes enough knowledge of nutrition to make informed personal choices about diet and health. Agriculturally literate people would have the practical knowledge needed to care for their outdoor environments, which include lawns, gardens, recreational areas, and parks.

FINDINGS, CONCLUSIONS, AND RECOMMENDATIONS

In its analysis of the status of agricultural literacy, the committee found a number of disturbing trends. The committee recommends that each school, school district, and state assess the status of its existing programs and implement the recommendations it considers appropriate.

EDUCATION ABOUT AGRICULTURE

• **Most Americans know very little about agriculture, its social and economic significance in the United States, and particularly, its links to human health and environmental quality.**
• **Few systematic educational efforts are made to teach or otherwise develop agricultural literacy in students of any age. Although children are taught something about agriculture, the material tends to be fragmented, frequently outdated, usually only farm oriented, and often negative or condescending in tone.**

Systematic surveys, anecdotal evidence, testimony presented to the committee, and the experiences of committee members strongly support the finding that current levels of agricultural literacy are low. The majority of American children enter school knowing little about agriculture and leave after high school graduation only slightly better informed.

In a study of the agricultural knowledge of 2,000 elementary, junior, and senior high students in Kansas, which is a major agricultural state, fewer than 30 percent of the students gave correct answers to relatively basic questions (Horn and Vining, 1986). Only 27.3 percent of the elementary school students knew that veal is the meat of young cattle; 25 percent of middle and junior high students knew that the sprouting of seeds is called germination; and 10 percent of senior high students knew that beef cattle production was the primary industry in Kansas in terms of gross sales. In many cases, the majority of students chose to answer, "I don't know."

In Virginia, students in 244 fourth-grade classrooms had only a rudimentary concept of where their food and fiber originate (Oliver, 1986). Nor are they curious to find out: teachers estimated that students asked questions about agriculture near the "almost never" end of a five-point scale of frequency.

One parent summarized the situation well. "Agriculture is not stressed in the school systems whatsoever. This is easily seen in all three of my children, who get precious little in the way of discussion of agriculture or what it means to modern society from kindergarten to high school" (Heath, 1986).

But the teaching of agricultural literacy need not require major curriculum reform. It will require innovative, classroom-tested materials, however. Children can plant radishes in a science class one week, and harvest them a few weeks later. A biology course that already includes modules on genetics could readily be taught with some agricultural examples. Students could learn from examples dealing with production differences among major crops, such as wheat, soybeans, corn, and vegetables. In a plant pathology module, students could learn about major crop diseases and the role of insects in disease transmission. Classroom discussion of topical issues, such as biotechnology, could greatly increase student interest in basic scientific concepts. The study of food and agriculture encompasses production, trade, processing, distribution, and marketing. This offers an opportunity to teach social science topics such as economics, civics, governmental operations, sociology, and managerial science as well as issues that relate to nutrition, famine, and obesity. In history class, students can study not only the expeditions, voyages, wars, and treaties through which new lands were acquired, but they can also read about how pioneer families grew their first crops, transforming the new lands into a nation. Mathematics courses, particularly computer exercises, could include many interesting examples from agriculture, foods, and nutrition.

This approach can be flexible according to the varying needs and resources in individual schools across the country. A program in Missoula, Montana, that focuses on forestry, trout fishing, and the lives of grizzly bears may be less meaningful—and less effective—when used with children in inner-city Boston. There, how the fishing industry operates might be of greater interest.

• **All students should receive at least some systematic instruction about agriculture beginning in kindergarten or first grade and continuing through twelfth grade. Much of the material** could be incorporated into existing courses and would not have to be taught separately.

• State education leaders, school administrators, and school boards should develop and implement a plan to foster instruction about the food and fiber system and its history, role in advancing science and technology, and regional significance in selected areas of the curriculum.

• Teachers should be encouraged to modify lesson plans to incorporate materials about scientific, economic, and public health aspects of agriculture and related topics in accordance with school policy. To accomplish the goal of agricultural literacy, teachers need resources and support.

• Representatives of agribusiness, particularly at the local and state levels, and community leaders should meet with school officials to implement cooperative efforts to bring more agriculture into the curriculum.

• Senior government officials and political leaders in the U.S. Departments of Education and Agriculture must direct efforts to upgrade agricultural literacy to all state departments of education. These efforts should be reinforced by a commitment of resources that reach teachers.

• Curriculum development projects funded by the National Science Foundation (NSF) and U.S. Department of Education (USDE) should include the development of instructional modules and material leading to agricultural literacy. Officials responsible for ongoing project oversight should work toward this goal.

• National agricultural community and vocational education organizations should develop new links with national education, teacher, and environmental education organizations, with a goal of facilitating progress in the teaching of agricultural literacy.

TEACHING SCIENCE THROUGH AGRICULTURE

All students need an understanding of basic science concepts. Teaching science through agriculture would incorporate more agriculture into curricula, while more effectively teaching science.

There are many opportunities to teach science through agriculture. A common way to capture student interest in science is often by reference to examples in the real world. Teachers can illustrate these examples by bringing an aspect of a living, natural system into the classroom for experimentation and observation.

Many have noted the deficiencies in science education in the United States in terms of student preparation and performance (National

Academies of Sciences and Engineering, 1982). Inadequate science education has been a cause of concern in the nation's efforts to sustain international competitiveness. As a result of this concern, high school students in thousands of schools are now required to take two science classes. Federal and state agencies have increased science curriculum development efforts and in-service education.

Less progress has been made in elementary schools, however, because teachers generally have little time left after covering the required core curriculum. Introducing instruction about agriculture as a separate subject in the elementary school curriculum would worsen existing time pressures and would not be welcomed by teachers or principals.

Curriculum integration is a more reasonable approach to achieve the agricultural literacy goal. By incorporating agriculture into existing subjects in the core curriculum, such as science, time pressures need not be aggravated. The Life Lab Science Program is an example. Life Lab began in 1978 as one teacher's special project at Green Acres Elementary School in Santa Cruz, California. More than 100 elementary

PHOTOGRAPH: WENDY FELTHAM

Life Lab students display pride in their "Growing Classroom." More than 100 schools nationwide use the award-winning science/nutrition/gardening program, which was recently granted $2.1 million from the National Science Foundation.

schools across the nation now use the program. The California School Boards Association and the National Science Teachers Association have named it a model program (Feltham, 1986). The National Science Foundation recently awarded Life Lab a $2.1 million grant to develop a comprehensive elementary science curriculum (Life Lab Science Program, 1988).

Life Lab is designed to give elementary school children an awareness and understanding of science and nutrition through the process of growing and tending a garden. The material is divided into three volumes, *The Growing Classroom* (Jaffe et al., 1985), that teachers have developed and tested. Children learn about soil, photosynthesis, interdependency, energy, pest management, and recycling, among other topics. With the garden as the living laboratory, they learn to solve problems, cooperate, observe, keep records, and think logically. The knowledge and skills children gain in Life Lab serve them long after they leave the elementary school garden.

Life Lab has measurable effects on children's knowledge. Green Acres students showed continual growth in science achievement at every grade level on the science portion of the Standardized and Comprehensive Test of Basic Skills (Feltham, 1986).

In many elementary schools, the most realistic way to teach science through agriculture is to introduce modules, or units of instruction, that supplement and eventually replace existing curricula and textbooks. A number of school districts have implemented hands-on elementary science programs using this approach; teachers are provided with four to six teaching modules per year. Each module focuses on a particular science topic and provides teachers with the instructional materials and apparatus needed to investigate the topic in the classroom, as well as lesson plans for 6 to 8 weeks of instruction.

Many school districts that use this approach successfully do not rely on elementary science texts produced by commercial publishers. Instead, they adapt a variety of nationally and locally produced materials to their needs. [One example of this is *The Science Workbook of Student Research Projects in Food–Agriculture–Natural Resources*, produced by faculty in the Ohio State University's College of Agriculture for secondary school students (Darrow, 1985). The projects are geared to give students hands-on experience.] These districts minimize the cost of materials by producing their own science apparatus kits for each module, refurbishing and recycling them so several teachers each year can use each kit (National Science Resources Center, 1986).

The average elementary school teacher has a limited background in science. A recent survey found, however, that the majority of elementary school teachers enjoy teaching science (Weiss, 1987). Elementary science in-service education programs would benefit many teachers. In-service education in science can be most effectively structured around a series of workshops, each one addressing a particular science topic or instructional module (National Science Resources Center, 1986).

The National Science Resources Center, a promising new effort jointly sponsored by the Smithsonian Institution and National Academy of Sciences, is currently working to improve the teaching of science in the nation's elementary schools. The center's Science and Technology for Children curriculum development project will produce a set of hands-on elementary science modules, develop improved models for in-service teacher education, and provide leadership training and technical assistance to school systems. This project will place a special emphasis on serving urban school districts with large minority populations. Some of the Science and Technology for Children elementary science modules will focus on topics related to agriculture.

Life and earth science courses in junior high include material about physiology, nutrition, plants and animals, taxonomic classification, soil formation, the hydrogeological cycle, and other topics that contribute to agricultural literacy.

The most significant opportunity after junior high for teaching science through agriculture comes in biology. This course is usually taught in the ninth grade. It is the one high school science class nearly all students take.

Biology courses and textbooks include many topics directly related to agriculture. A few major biology textbooks dominate the marketplace. Hence, if instructional materials developed for use with these texts were well received by teachers and readily available, they could reach a high percentage of students. The committee reviewed one widely used biology textbook and identified the following units as suited to the teaching of science through agriculture (Otto and Towle, 1985).

- **Applied genetics: classical applied genetics, plant and animal breeding, and molecular biology and recombinant DNA.**
- **Bacteria: the nitrogen cycle, beneficial uses of bacteria in food production, food spoilage, formation of genetic resistance to drugs or pesticides, and advice for the safe handling of food.**
- **Multicellular plants: plant structure and function and the biology of trees.**
- **Invertebrates and vertebrates: insects and other arthropods, parasites, earthworms, fishes, birds, and mammals; and the relationships of these animals to humans.**

- **Ecological relationships: ecosystems, populations, communities, and the genesis of environmental problems.**

The committee believes it is unrealistic to expect school districts—with a few exceptions—to redesign curricula at any grade level to make agriculture a major focus. But it also believes that many science educators recognize merit in the use of well-designed, scientifically sound modules addressing real world problems and applications and their scientific and technological components. Agricultural and scientific literacy are enhanced when closely related in school.

The following steps should be taken to improve science education:

- **Science teachers and specialists with a knowledge of agriculture involved in curriculum development projects, including those funded by the NSF, should examine existing textbooks and curricula to identify opportunities to incorporate subject matter from the plant, animal, ecological, and nutritional sciences. Instructional material should be designed to give students an interest in and increasing understanding of human ecology and the agricultural food and fiber system.**
- **The National Science Teachers Association should help to identify and disseminate information on effective methods and materials that teach science through agriculture.**
- **School district, state department of education, and teacher education personnel should conduct and participate in professional development activities with teachers. These activities would focus on the integration of agriculture into the curriculum.**
- **Curriculum design and in-service education opportunities need to evolve together.**
- **Special applied science courses on agricultural topics should be available as optional elective science courses for those students who wish to go beyond the traditional science course curriculum. Such courses, when designed and taught with an acceptable level of scientifically relevant content, should earn full academic credit toward graduation and college entrance requirements.**

TEACHER EDUCATION AND TRAINING

- **Virtually no effort is made anywhere to educate teachers about agriculture, except for the teacher education programs designed for vocational agriculture teachers.**
- **Some instructional materials that address aspects of agri-**

cultural literacy are available in each state to augment several
required academic courses. This material is uneven in quality
and rarely used to full advantage, however. Teachers are generally unaware of how to secure better materials or receive help
in the use of available instructional materials.

Participants in public meetings told the committee that teachers
have little opportunity to learn about agriculture in their professional
preparation or in-service education. Courses imparting the concepts
and knowledge integral to agricultural literacy are not available for
those preparing to teach, other than courses for individuals entering
vocational careers. In some states, teachers of vocational agriculture
are trained in a program within a college of agriculture; in other states,
these teachers are trained within a college of education. In either case,
there should be interaction between educators and agriculturists on
the same campus.

It is rare for high school vocational agriculture teachers to help their
colleagues incorporate instruction about agriculture into history, science, languages, and other courses. The reverse is also true. The committee was impressed with the positive response of teachers and students in some schools where vocational and academic teachers did work
together in this way. The coordination of overlapping classes between vocational agriculture and other teachers should involve joint registration
whenever possible. In a school in a midwestern state, for example, students who enroll in a trigonometry class also sign up for farm mechanics.

Teachers may also cooperate in common projects as well as in-class
teaching activities. The greenhouse energy conservation project at Anderson Valley High School, Boonville, California, is an example. Mathematics, science, computer, fine arts, and agriculture classes are involved in this project. Students are often in more than one of the
classes, which helps them to understand each subject's applications
more clearly.

One way to help teachers incorporate instruction about agriculture
is to make sure they know about existing programs and materials.
Practical examples and exercises that teachers can use to make abstract concepts and principles come alive for students should be emphasized. By taking advantage of what is already available, costs to
bring new materials into more classrooms could be kept to a minimum.
Cooperative ventures and partnerships among schools, businesses, cooperative extension, and colleges of agriculture might also reduce costs.

• **Administrators of teacher education programs and schools
of education should offer units of instruction or courses about
agriculture.**

- In-service education or special summer programs for teachers should be offered focusing on how to use new instructional material and take advantage of students' interest in agricultural subjects.
- Agribusinesses and teacher organizations should sponsor public service announcements in education journals or computer networks advising teachers where exemplary materials to teach agriculture can be obtained.
- Through letters to education journals, teachers should share with their colleagues ideas they have developed and curriculum materials on agriculture and related topics they have found helpful.
- The U.S. Department of Agriculture (USDA); the USDE; teacher organizations; agricultural organizations, such as the American Farm Bureau Federation and the National Grange; and state departments of agriculture and education should publish and disseminate curriculum materials on agriculture and related topics.
- Agricultural educators should serve on mathematics and science textbook preparation and selection committees; mathematics and science educators should likewise participate in choosing and revising agricultural texts and other instructional materials.
- A private national foundation, partially supported with public funds, should be established to produce and disseminate instructional materials on agricultural topics.
- Teachers in colleges of education should meet regularly with their counterparts in colleges of agriculture to explore setting up links between various programs. Private sector and legislative leaders should facilitate these interactions.
- Cooperative extension in each state needs to develop better networks between classroom teachers and active researchers and extension scientists knowledgeable about local agricultural production activities and the sciences basic to agriculture.
- Vocational agriculture directors should consider working with cooperative extension to develop local applied research.
- Teachers, school administrators, and curriculum specialists will need technical and financial support to develop and acquire new instructional materials.

MODEL PROGRAMS

- The Ag in the Classroom program and other efforts have produced useful materials and approaches at the elementary

and high school levels that could be used as models to improve education about contemporary agriculture.

• Students who have opportunities to join organizations like the National FFA (Future Farmers of America) Organization and 4-H can gain experience and knowledge by participating in special projects.

Incorporating agricultural literacy initiatives into the already full high school agenda is a difficult task. Neither educators nor parents universally agree that there is a need for agricultural literacy initiatives. School system administrators and teachers face many other priorities. Time is the most limiting resource—time to learn and prepare to teach a new subject area and to incorporate agricultural education into the curriculum. For these reasons, it is important to build on and replicate in other schools successful agricultural education initiatives that are now in place.

One such successful program centered principally in elementary school is the Ag in the Classroom program. The USDA began the program in 1981 through state departments of agriculture or state Farm Bureau organizations. Ag in the Classroom has already demonstrated the potential benefits from properly structured initiatives. It is the most extensive effort under way to make elementary school students more knowledgeable about the food and fiber system. It works by incorporating agricultural instructional material and subject matter into classroom activities. The USDA acts as an information clearinghouse and resource to encourage states and school districts to adopt the program. Districts in the program provide in-service training opportunities and special instructional material to teachers, who then pursue a variety of options for incorporating new subject matter into the curriculum.

The variety of materials produced for the Ag in the Classroom program reflects diverse efforts. In Oregon, an elementary school textbook was developed to teach the history and geography of the state through descriptions of its agriculture, timber, water, and wildlife. A companion textbook for high school students was developed that examines Oregon's role in the global economy, emphasizing the marketing process of the state's agricultural commodities (USDA, 1988). In Massachusetts, the Ag in the Classroom program has produced curriculum modules about the state's agriculture for integration into economics, nutrition, science, and social science classes in grades four through six (Garner-Koech, 1985). Arkansas and Illinois have cooperated on the development of curriculum modules for all grade levels that focus on the economics of the American and international agricultural systems (USDA, 1988).

Forty-seven states have developed materials as part of the Ag in the Classroom program. In most cases, the materials span several school grades. In 38 states, a combined total of 21,000 teachers have been prepared in the use of Ag in the Classroom materials. As a conservative estimate, these teachers have reached more than 1.2 million students (USDA, 1988).

The FFA is a successful student organization integrated with most vocational agriculture programs. Food for America, an FFA program, provides opportunities for students not enrolled in vocational agriculture to receive agriculture-related instruction. This program encourages FFA members to visit elementary schools to discuss with children the importance of food and agribusiness. And a private association of scientific societies and individual agricultural scientists, the Council for Agricultural Science and Technology, distributes to about 16,000 high school science departments a free quarterly newsletter, *Science of Food and Agriculture*. Beginning in the fall of 1988, teachers will be surveyed on their use of this newsletter.

The Cooperative Extension System (CES), a consortium of USDA's Extension Service and land-grant universities, oversees the 4-H youth education program. This program contributes to agricultural literacy through informal educational program activities. During 1986, about 8.5 million young people were involved with individual 4-H projects. Of these projects, 88 percent were scientific in content; 55 percent of the total were based in the biological sciences (USDA, 1987).

An individual or group CES 4-H project usually entails making or growing something. Projects in the biological sciences can supplement classroom instruction. Members enrolled in gardening projects learn about plant and soil science, tool selection and use, ecological cycles, and how humans can alter the landscape. A CES 4-H dairy foods project designed for 4-H members in their early teens incorporates information about nutrition, health and fitness, and consumer skills needed to buy and prepare food.

The CES also makes instructional materials designed to enrich school curricula available as part of 4-H activities. These materials reach a surprisingly large number of students. About 2.1 million 4-H participants are involved in 51,000 class instructional units (USDA, 1987). While information on measurable benefits is limited, a recent USDA report cites some significant results (USDA, 1987). Third-, fourth-, and fifth-grade students in 4-H were tested before and after an urban forestry program. On a quantitative scale representing level of knowledge, the average increase in understanding about forestry among the 400 participating pupils was estimated to be 65 percent. Like other programs, the value of a student's 4-H experience depends on a number

At the Wisconsin State Extension Service's Farm Progress Days, 4-H'ers demonstrate food preparation. Members of 4-H may choose projects from many program areas, including food and nutrition; natural resources; economics; jobs and careers; and communications arts and sciences.

of factors—commitment of teachers, relevance and integration in the academic curriculum, parental involvement, and community support.

• **Ag in the Classroom state coordinators should build new linkages with science, mathematics, and vocational agriculture teachers; state departments and colleges of agriculture and education; agribusiness; farm groups; and 4-H and other CES personnel. The program needs more support at the national and state levels to accomplish these goals.**

• **State vocational agriculture supervisors, other education leaders, and state agriculture and education department officials should encourage use of proven instructional programs like 4-H and Ag in the Classroom for students in grades kindergarten through 12.**

COMMUNITY INVOLVEMENT

• **The integration of agriculture in the curricula of school districts reflects a broad base of community interest and support.**

Formal and informal cooperation is needed among all organizations within a community to contribute to education in and about agriculture. One example of cooperation is Building Our American Communities (BOAC), a community development program involving more than 4,406 local FFA chapters. In BOAC, FFA members and advisers work in cooperation with local leaders to identify special community needs. The cooperative effort allows FFA members to apply the competencies and skills learned in the vocational agriculture classroom. New BOAC priorities include marketing, agricultural technology, international relations, and economic development.

In attempting to discover why some communities and schools give agriculture much more emphasis than other communities, the committee identified several possible variables: availability of good instructional materials, teacher initiative and interest, and leadership and cooperation among teachers, school administrators, CES personnel, and volunteers. In the manner of agricultural extension agents, education agents may be needed to work with communities.

At the annual National 4-H Invitational Conference, 4-H members participate in activities designed to broaden their knowledge of conservation practices and forestry management. Here, participants study tree measurements to estimate the amount of various products that might be cut from the tree.

• Teachers and school officials need to know the views of parents and local leaders regarding the adequacy of instruction in and about agriculture. Teachers and school officials are more likely to act on expressed concerns backed by offers of help in developing or obtaining special instructional material.

AGRICULTURAL CAREER EXPLORATION PROGRAMS

• In junior high school, career exploration programs in agriculture are rare. The Hereford Middle School in Monkton, Maryland, offers one such program.

• Neither students nor Americans in general have a realistic view of agriculture's scope, career possibilities, or involvement with scientific progress and the use of sophisticated biological, chemical, mechanical, and electronic technologies.

In early stages of their education, students need to be aware of career possibilities. Many students make their first decisions about career options in middle school or junior high school, when they choose courses that will help prepare them for a cluster of career choices. In some subjects, such as foreign languages and home economics, students are given an idea of job possibilities through short career exploration programs.

The first step in career exploration is making students aware of the diversity of possible careers within broad fields of endeavor. Few schools have agriculture and food industry exploration programs, perhaps because most Americans associate agriculture exclusively with farming. A recent Gallup poll showed that Americans esteem agriculture and farming, but would not choose farming as a career for themselves or their children (AGFOCUS: A Project of America's Governors, Inc., 1986). They perceive it as hard, risky work with little economic return.

Students hold similar opinions. A study for the University of California at Davis of high school juniors' and seniors' college preparatory curricula found that students identified agriculture solely with farming (Mallory and Sommer, 1986a,b). Synonymous with farming were the words outdoor, hard work, male, boring, and insecure. They rated a career in agriculture high for the opportunity to contribute to society and to be one's own boss, but very low to provide for a secure future and in terms of earning potential.

Many people are unaware of how rapidly the food and agricultural sciences are progressing. Because of this progress, many different professional careers have evolved in support of the less than 3 percent of the nation's labor force that are farmers working in production agriculture. Nearly 20 percent of the labor force works for the agricultural industry in some capacity. The food retailing industry, restaurants, and cafeterias in private and public institutions employ around 12 percent of these workers (Petrulis et al., 1987). Others are employed in occupations related to the management of natural and human environments. Some examples of these occupations are landscape architecture, urban erosion control, care of parks and golf courses, microbiology, and nutrition. Those who work in these fields have generally received their professional and technical training in agricultural sciences and technology.

Another myth that career exploration programs need to dismiss is that everyone involved with agriculture is suffering economic stress and faces bleak prospects for future growth. Several food, fiber, and agricultural industries are profitable and growing. Examples of growth are in food processing and agricultural service industries. Economic opportunities await companies that can take advantage of new and growing markets, such as the market for nonfood uses of agricultural products. A wide range of job opportunities for individuals with some education in agriculture—from high school diplomas to Ph.D. degrees—exist in research, agribusiness management and marketing, education, foreign service, and civil service professions and occupations. (For a more detailed review of these professions, see Coulter et al., 1986.)

Located in an almost entirely rural school district north of Baltimore, the Hereford Middle School has developed the Agribusiness-Technology Studies Program for seventh- and eighth-grade students. The school has also developed a related course in biotechnology for advanced eighth-grade students. These mandatory courses are designed to inform students about careers, instill agricultural and environmental literacy, improve academic skills, and promote responsibility and public service.

All seventh-grade students are required to complete the 19-week course, which meets three times a week. During that time, they learn about the historical development of agribusiness and technology and their effect on the evolution of society. The applied part of the course covers plant and animal science; garden tractor safety and operation; resource conservation, measurement, and planning; woodworking; public speaking; and parliamentary procedures. Computers are used in various parts of the course.

The course for eighth-grade students, which is also 19 weeks, focuses on current and future agricultural practices. The applied part of the course covers career research and exploration, entrepreneurship and occupational studies, plastic working, floral design, gardening, computer programming as a basic language, landscaping, and landscape design. The biotechnology course covers many of these subjects. It also examines hydroponics, tissue culture, genetic engineering, and computer applications (F. H. Doepkens, Hereford Middle School, personal communication, 1988).

The Hereford school program is suited to the needs of its district. But a city school might want to emphasize careers more common in urban areas, such as food science, nutrition and dietary planning and counseling, marketing, and the like. In rural areas, where students may have grown up on farms, program planners and counselors face different challenges in broadening students' perceptions of agricultural career opportunities.

The committee was impressed with the opportunities to use advanced telecommunication and video equipment to provide students information on careers in agriculture. Many schools effectively use video discs, cassettes, and other audiovisual materials in structured and unstructured career counseling sessions. Schools can supplement use of these materials at little or no cost by inviting guest speakers representing various parts of the agricultural industry to visit classes.

Audiovisual material can bring students into the laboratories, factories, and fields where agricultural and food science technology is under development. Audiovisual material can also show students practical problems such as dry stream beds, blowing soil, or a field of lettuce destroyed by insects. Students can then be challenged to think what solutions they might help to discover if trained as an engineer, microbiologist, or public policy specialist.

In career exploration program initiatives, educators should tailor program content to the needs and circumstances of different segments within the school population. Educators should be particularly alert to the interests of girls and minority students because both groups are underrepresented in most agricultural careers. Urban students are often overlooked by agricultural educators. All of these students need new materials and nontraditional role models to help to generate their interest in agricultural and food industry careers. Last, teachers and counselors in rural and urban schools should collaborate to combine aspects of career exploration programs with other initiatives to advance agricultural literacy.

- **The unique needs and career prospects of students at each school in different regions should be considered when developing agricultural exploration programs.**
- **Career exploration programs need to emphasize professional agricultural careers to a greater degree, showing the connection between college preparation and agricultural leadership, business, and scientific occupations.**

3

Vocational Agriculture Education

Vocational agriculture has a long history in American education. By those who were enrolled as students, vocational agriculture remains one of the most widely praised secondary school programs in the country. Most programs consist of three parts: classroom and laboratory instruction, supervised occupational experiences (SOEs), and membership in the FFA. Vocational agriculture can be a demanding and rewarding program. Students and teachers spend considerable time in and outside school following the curriculum and working on projects.

When federally supported vocational agriculture education was created in 1917, about one-third of the U.S. population lived on farms. Farm businesses dominated rural life and sustained rural communities. Today, the U.S. farm population is about 2.2 percent of the overall population. Technological evolution over the last half century has transformed the nature and vastly broadened the range of agricultural occupations and professional careers. U.S. industries that serve agriculture by producing, processing, marketing, and preparing food and fiber products for consumers account for about $700 billion in economic activity each year, which is about 16.5 percent of the gross national product (U.S. Departments of Agriculture and Commerce, 1986; U.S. Department of Commerce Bureau of the Census, 1988).

The economic crisis in farming has affected vocational agriculture education programs, particularly in regions where bad weather and weak commodity markets have been problems since 1980. Students who once might have followed their parents into farming, or worked in a farm-related service industry or business often now have little interest in agriculture. Some parents with farm backgrounds encourage their children to pursue other careers. The media have exposed students from families not associated with farming to the often highly visible problems in farming. Considering evidence cited in Chapter 2 that most Americans perceive agriculture and farming as synonymous, it is not surprising that many students are uninterested or skeptical when evaluating opportunities that might follow from enrollment in a vocational agriculture program.

FINDINGS, CONCLUSIONS, AND RECOMMENDATIONS

Change within agriculture is an ongoing process that will affect agricultural businesses and institutions. They must adapt to continue serving agriculture. The institution of vocational agriculture education is no exception.

PROGRAM ENROLLMENT AND AVAILABILITY

Enrollment

Enrollments in vocational agriculture programs peaked in the late 1970s and are now declining about 1 to 3 percent annually. Figures 3-1 and 3-2 show the decline of agriculture enrollments compared with other vocational education courses.

Based on the analysis of data and testimony presented by several experts, the committee finds:

- **Less than 5 percent of the high school population enrolls in a 3- or 4-year vocational agriculture education program.**
- **The number of viable programs nationwide is declining; consequently, the number of students served by such programs is declining.**

Little is known about vocational agriculture enrollment trends. The USDE no longer collects data on students taking vocational agriculture courses.

Enrollment data that are available are often difficult to interpret, aggregate, or compare over time because of different definitions, sampling techniques, and reporting requirements. Nonetheless, the available evidence is adequate to reach some general judgments about the availability and enrollments in vocational agriculture programs among high school students.

The committee believes that the best estimates of enrollment trends in vocational agriculture programs can be extrapolated from statistics on FFA membership. This organization has compiled records for nearly six decades, using a relatively consistent methodology. The National FFA Center compiles the data that state supervisors of agriculture have collected (National FFA Organization, 1986). Drawing on state surveys of vocational agriculture teachers, the FFA estimates that about 75 percent of vocational agriculture students are FFA members. This percentage appears to have remained roughly constant over the last few decades.

Enrollment in vocational agriculture programs for full-time secondary school students grew quickly in the 1930s, rising from about 123,685 in 1930 to 329,398 in 1940. In the next decade, enrollment expanded to approximately 376,897. The 1950s brought much slower growth; enrollments stood at 463,960 in 1960. In the 1960s, enrollment continued to increase, although somewhat erratically (Roberts, 1971). Another steady growth phase began in 1971, which approximately paralleled the expansion in agricultural production and profits during the 1970s.

Peak enrollments probably occurred in 1976 to 1977, when about 697,500 students were enrolled in vocational agriculture programs (National FFA Organization, 1986). This was about 5 percent of the 14.5 million students in high school. In 1986, vocational agriculture enrollment had declined to about 525,071. FFA membership followed a similar pattern, declining from 507,735 members in 1976–1977 to 430,184 members in 1985–1986. Of these 430,184 students, 113,317 were from the FFA's Central Region (Illinois, Indiana, Iowa, Kansas, Kentucky, Michigan, Minnesota, Missouri, Nebraska, North Dakota, South Dakota, and Wisconsin); 77,836 were from the Eastern Region (Connecticut, Delaware, Maine, Maryland, Massachusetts, New Hampshire, New Jersey, New York, North Carolina, Ohio, Pennsylvania, Rhode Island, Vermont, Virginia, and West Virginia); 106,338 were from the Southern Region (Alabama, Arkansas, Florida, Georgia, Louisiana, Mississippi, Puerto Rico, South Carolina, and Tennessee); and 132,693 were from the Western Region (Alaska, Arizona, California, Hawaii, Idaho, Montana, Nevada, New Mexico, Oklahoma, Oregon, Texas, Utah, Washington, and Wyoming). The high school population also declined over this period, falling to about 12.4 million students in 1986 (USDE, 1987). Vocational agriculture program enrollment currently is about 4.5 percent of the high school population (National FFA Organization, 1986).

Availability

Vocational agriculture is most commonly found in general or comprehensive high schools; in 1985, 77.7 percent of vocational agriculture high school teaching positions were in such schools (Camp, 1987). Other programs are based in vocational schools, including 2-year postsecondary technical centers. In more than half the schools, one teacher is responsible for vocational agriculture programs (Camp, 1987). About 35 percent of the programs are in schools located in 13 southern states: Alabama, Arkansas, Florida, Georgia, Kentucky, Louisiana, Mississippi, North Carolina, Oklahoma, South Carolina, Tennessee, Texas, and Virginia. Some people believe the South has a disproportionately high number of vocational agriculture programs. The reasons for this are agriculture is economically important in the South, social and cultural conditions create expectations for the schools to teach vocations, and many Southerners practice small-farm agriculture as a way of life (Lee, 1986).

The committee found few convincing studies and data on why some school districts offer vocational agriculture, while others do not, or why vocational programs do well in some schools, but are weak in others nearby. One study of Kansas school districts without vocational agri-

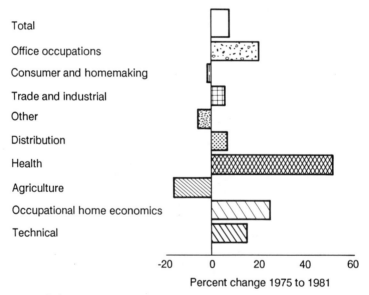

FIGURE 3-1 Change in vocational education enrollments (in percent). SOURCE: USDE, 1983.

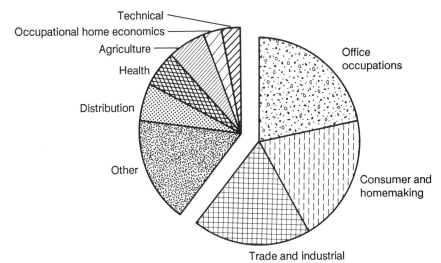

FIGURE 3-2 Distribution in vocational education enrollments.
SOURCE: USDE, 1983.

culture found that rural residents and agribusiness representatives wanted such programs, but school administrators did not. The administrators cited a lack of student interest, facilities, money, and need for vocational agriculture (Parmley, 1982).

Minority Enrollments

Historically, vocational agriculture has been most attractive to white male students in rural areas. Enrollment trends show that more girls are now enrolling in vocational agriculture, but minority enrollment remains disproportionately low. The committee identified several possible reasons for relatively low minority and female enrollment in vocational agriculture programs.

Many farming communities where vocational agriculture is most common are still predominantly white. Black and other minority students, such as those of Hispanic or Asian origins, in many states and most urban areas have little exposure to agriculture or agriculture education. In a survey conducted by the University of California at Davis, black students questioned for a survey gave two main reasons for their lack of interest in agriculture: they didn't know much about the agricultural system, and what they did know led them to view agriculture as a financially risky line of work (Mallory and Sommer, 1986a,b). Some black students may avoid vocational agriculture because of its association with slavery. Vocational agriculture may not attract blacks and Hispanics because they have traditionally held low-paying menial jobs in agriculture.

Vocational agriculture educators know they need to improve their efforts to reach minority students. As one California educator explained to the committee:

We're headed for a change in California's minority population and what we are doing is not working. Agriculture has a big negative image problem with most minority groups and we have to change it. It needs to start in grammar school and be nurtured through high school. (Bowen, 1986)

Vocational agriculture educators also need to reach disadvantaged and disabled students.

Female enrollment in vocational agriculture varies from school district to school district and program to program. It is common to find relatively high percentages of girls enrolled in horticulture courses within vocational agriculture programs; in some states and school districts, a higher percentage of girls are enrolling in these courses than in recent years. In California, not only were far more females enrolling in vocational agriculture (girls accounted for 39.2 percent of FFA membership in a recent survey), but they also held 45.2 percent of the chapter offices (Leising and Emo, 1984). Nationally, girls account for about 15 percent of FFA membership; about half the number of high school students are girls. Progress is being made in some states, especially in the Northeast, to open up both the FFA and vocational agriculture programs to nontraditional enrollees.

Neither the testimony heard by the committee nor available studies explain why female enrollment has grown so much in some states and chapters. One plausible explanation is that ornamental horticulture is a very attractive career in urban and suburban areas. Research on the question is neither clear nor consistent. Some studies show that girls were encouraged to enter vocational agriculture programs, while others found they were discouraged (Parmley et al., 1981; Higgins, 1984).

Most states should make stronger recruitment efforts to bring more minority and female students into vocational agriculture programs. These students need to be alerted to educational choices within the school and career opportunities in food, agriculture, and related industries and occupations.

Demographics affect challenges faced by vocational agriculture educators in different parts of the country. In the South, for example, where about 85 percent of the nation's black farmers live, the continued decline of land ownership and control of farm operations by blacks is a serious concern (U.S. Commission on Civil Rights, 1982). There and elsewhere, agricultural educators must be especially sensitive to the needs of all students and the community.

Some minority students also have special educational needs in academic subjects and vocational courses. Vocational agriculture teachers need to accommodate diverse educational needs.

The creation of vocational agriculture programs in schools where none exist calls for policy incentives. These incentives are especially important in urban communities where most of the minority population lives.

• **Vocational agriculture educators in communities with minority students should establish new links with underrepresented groups of students through community leaders; churches; and local organizations, such as the Boy Scouts, Girl Scouts, and 4-H. Minority business people and employers should be encouraged to help create new supervised occupational experience programs.**

• **The local news media and FFA publications and chapter and state meetings should continue to feature female and minority students who have won achievements and honors.**

• **In setting the future course for vocational agriculture education, education leaders should consider demographic trends in a region's total population, farm population, food and fiber industries, and other employment opportunities in the service or business sectors related to agriculture.**

PROGRAM CONTENT

The Current Curriculum

In content, the vocational agriculture curriculum has failed to keep up with modern agriculture. More flexibility in curriculum and program design and the requirements and activities of the FFA is essential. One educator's analysis is typical of statements heard repeatedly by the committee:

In spite of the rhetoric of the profession that we are not training primarily for farming occupations and that agriculture education has changed dramatically, the typical agriculture program remains much as it was when the Vocational Education Act of 1963 was passed. Production agriculture, taught by a single teacher, in a general high school, remains the norm. (Camp, 1986)

The production focus of most vocational agriculture programs can be traced, in part, to two studies that widely influenced vocational curricula across the nation. In 1977, Iowa State University, under the sponsorship of the U.S. Office of Education, conducted a study to specify standards for quality programs of vocational agriculture (Standards for Quality Vocational Programs in Agriculture/Agribusiness Education, 1977). Many states subsequently adopted the recommendations in the Iowa study, which emphasized production agriculture subjects. A nationwide competency study in 1978 also played a key role (McClay, 1978). It was conducted to identify and validate competencies needed for entry and advancement in 196 agriculture and agribusiness occupations. Traditional agricultural programs and occupations dominated the findings and recommendations, which in turn affected curriculum design in vocational agriculture programs across the country.

Available statistics on program subject matter also point to the dominance of production agriculture. In 1986, 40.7 percent of vocational agriculture teachers in secondary schools taught full-time in production agriculture programs; 30.0 percent were in part-time production agriculture programs with one or more classes in specialized programs, such as agricultural mechanics; and the remainder taught classes in ornamental horticulture, natural resources, agricultural products, agricultural sales and services, and agricultural mechanics (Camp, 1987).

Current vocational agriculture programs that have changed little over the past decade prepare students for a rather limited and generally shrinking component of the job market. These programs are also geared to a shrinking segment of the student population. They probably give some students an unrealistic view of agricultural job prospects, while failing to alert them to other career opportunities in agriculture.

New efforts are needed to reform secondary school agriculture programs to better prepare students for agricultural-sector growth industries. An essential step toward achieving this goal is to fully accept the broadened definition of agriculture education recommended by the committee. In some cases, this will require change in or abandonment of vocational guidelines. Under vocational agriculture, this definition would include greater diversity of career paths, such as scientific research, technology development, medical and social services, finance, law, business, management, and marketing.

• **The organization name, symbols, contests, awards, and requirements for advancement in the FFA are still largely geared toward production agriculture. Because the FFA influences vocational agriculture so greatly, some change within the FFA is needed along with program and curriculum reform. The curriculum should drive the youth organization, not the reverse.**

Uneven Quality

Although many more students have access to vocational agriculture programs than enroll in them, only a small percentage of schools offers students an opportunity to enroll in a high-quality vocational program. The characteristics of high-quality programs include extensive contact between students and teachers and a diversity of rewarding SOE opportunities.

The committee is aware of only a few states that have a routine process to evaluate the vocational curriculum or have quality control standards to identify and assess weaknesses within programs. California has developed such standards and a process for self-renewal that could serve as a model for consideration by other states.

In developing such standards, the accomplishments of high-quality programs should be studied and used as models, particularly those that give students educational experiences in many areas of agricultural business and science. Special agricultural science schools in Philadelphia and Chicago are valuable models for other cities and rural areas studying the feasibility of setting up science- and business-oriented programs.

Good programs attract a cross-section of the high school population, including student leaders and individuals bound for college. Poor programs suffer declining enrollments and rarely can hold the interest of students who are high achievers.

While good programs are generally expensive, poor programs tend to cost nearly as much or more on a per student basis. It is important to keep in mind that vocational agriculture is *not* the most expensive vocational education or basic education program in our schools. Despite growing pressures on school budgets, some communities continue to support weak programs because of their long-standing commitments to vocational agriculture and the FFA. These communities are often eager for new ideas and options that could strengthen agricultural education. Programs that are not meeting students' needs and lack community and school support are a poor use of resources. Steps should be taken to upgrade, consolidate, or, as a last resort, phase out such programs.

Care should be exercised in devising and implementing remedial strategies within a school district to assure that support and resources are not diverted from programs with capable teachers, sufficient enrollments, and community support. In fact, strong programs may deserve additional resources.

The committee emphasizes that strong programs are the result of strong teachers and support from principals and school district administrators. Innovation in program design and content typically occurs because a teacher chooses to go beyond the standard curriculum and program model and has the opportunity to do so. The current vocational structure and funding criteria do not sufficiently encourage innovation within the classroom, however, and can even penalize those trying to broaden the scope of the agricultural curriculum. Some of the most successful and innovative schools have even dropped the term "vocational" from their names and course titles because of their unwillingness or inability to function within the prescribed, traditional boundaries of vocational agriculture education. Federal and state laws and program criteria governing the allocation of vocational funds are responsible for these constraints.

• **State leaders must assist school boards, administrators, and local leaders to address the uneven quality of vocational agriculture programs and make available adequate resources to support recommended program improvements.**

Improving Quality

The committee found it easy to identify the reasons some vocational agriculture programs are weak. The absence of leadership among those responsible for vocational agriculture education programs is the primary cause of weak programs. The following steps must be taken to improve weak programs:

• **identify and define the problems and causes;**
• **develop a strategic plan to improve program quality;**
• **provide the resources to carry out the plan for improvement; and**
• **evaluate the results of the plan for improvement, and make necessary adjustments on a timely basis.**

Each school will experience different challenges and must develop its own strategy. These strategies include upgrading the vocational agriculture education program to attract higher levels of school, student, and community support; securing more competent teachers; upgrading the relevance of the curriculum; consolidation with a closely associated program or technical school in the same school district; and integrating agricultural subject matter into other components of the curriculum. In light of the emphasis and evidence that quality teachers are the critical ingredient for quality programs, adequate attention must be focused on teacher evaluation, in-service education, new curriculum directions, recruitment, and training.

- Successful reform efforts within vocational agriculture programs will rely on strong programmatic leadership at the state and national levels. The major leadership challenges include program evaluation, teacher education, curriculum development, assuring adequate resources at the local level, and creating a more flexible legislative and budgetary framework.

- Each school with a program in agriculture education should have an active advisory council comprised of school administrators; curriculum specialists; and local leaders in agricultural organizations, agribusiness, and public service.

- Ongoing efforts should be expanded and accelerated to upgrade the scientific and technical content of vocational agriculture courses. The "vocational" label should be avoided to help attract students with diverse interests, including the college bound and those aspiring to professional and scientific careers in agriculture. Agricultural courses sufficiently upgraded in science content should be credited toward satisfying college entrance and high school graduation requirements for science courses in addition to the core curriculum.

- New curriculum components must be developed and made available to teachers addressing the sciences basic to agriculture, food, and natural resources; agribusiness; marketing; management; international economics; financial accounting; and tools to improve the efficiency of agricultural productivity.

- A center for curriculum design and staff development involving faculty from colleges of agriculture and education should be established, preferably at the land-grant university in each state. Center staff should be available to provide direct help to local agriculture programs. Federal challenge grants should be provided to states ready and willing to take on this task.

- School district officials should find new methods of cooperation among those involved in teaching agriculture education, including secondary and postsecondary teachers, active parent volunteers, the CES and university experts, and organizations like 4-H and the FFA.

Model Programs

The committee identified several successful, high-quality, agriculture education programs that have combined strengths of the traditional vocational program model with new approaches and broadened curricula. Two are in specialized high schools of agriculture that also provide students with comprehensive instruction in other subjects.

Three others are in high schools that provide vocational agriculture programs.

At the Walter Biddle Saul High School of Agricultural Sciences in Philadelphia, juniors and seniors select one of seven agricultural areas in preparation for an occupation or admission to college (Walter Biddle Saul High School of Agricultural Sciences, 1980). The seven plans, which reflect all sectors of the agricultural industry, cover production, mechanics, products, horticulture, resources, animal technology, and business (Walter Biddle Saul High School of Agricultural Sciences, 1984). Laboratory instruction and experience are provided at the Fox

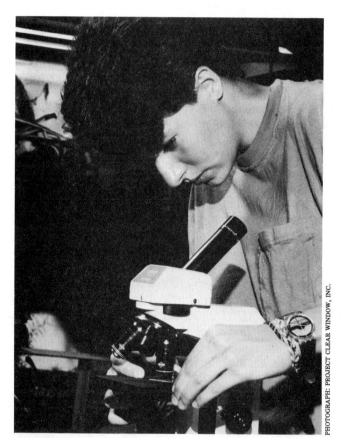

PHOTOGRAPH: PROJECT CLEAR WINDOW, INC.

A student adjusts a microscope in a science class at the Chicago High School for Agricultural Sciences. The school's curriculum, which is college preparatory and vocational at the same time, emphasizes science, mathematics, and computer education.

PHOTOGRAPH: PROJECT CLEAR WINDOW, INC.

Two students at the Chicago High School for Agricultural Sciences look over their flowers before the annual bedding plant sale, which is held in the community. The school prepares students to pursue career opportunities in horticulture, biotechnology, food science, agribusiness, commodities trading, golf course and greenhouse management, landscape design, and animal science.

Chase Farm located in a Philadelphia suburb and the city park system (Walter Biddle Saul High School of Agricultural Sciences, n.d.).

The Chicago High School for Agricultural Sciences is meeting a similar need. This magnet school began instruction in September 1985 (Russell, 1987). The curriculum is college preparatory and vocational at the same time. Agricultural science courses that mix science and more traditional vocational education include biotechnology; food, computer, plant, and animal sciences; agricultural finance; agribusiness; horticulture; landscape design; and golf course management. The curriculum places strong emphasis on basic intellectual and academic skills. In its first 2 years of operation, the school gained strong support from agribusiness leaders, parents, community members, and students. Student support was shown by the school's remarkable 93 percent attendance rate and zero dropout rate.

Job placement remains an important, although narrow criterion for judging vocational program effectiveness. The Chicago school is too new to evaluate in terms of job placements for graduates, but the Walter Biddle Saul High School has a good record (Hart, 1985). Employers from the Philadelphia area recruit graduates of this school. Job opportunities in horticulture; landscaping; and planning and maintaining parks, golf courses, and gardens are common (R. J. Hunter, Walter Biddle Saul High School of Agricultural Sciences, personal communication, 1988). Many graduates of the Walter Biddle Saul High School go on to college and careers in the agricultural sciences or other fields related to the food and fiber system. The committee views these specialized high schools as models for change and innovation, testing grounds for new ideas, and demonstrations of new programs in agriculture education.

Alvirne High School in Hudson, New Hampshire, offers another example of a vocational agriculture program that has adapted to meet the new needs of students. In the late 1960s, with the completion of the state's first interstate highway, the community was transformed from a farming area to a fast-growing suburb of Boston (Palmer, 1985). The vocational agriculture program was a one-teacher, traditional, production agriculture program.

Instead of abolishing vocational agriculture, the school district investigated alternative ways in which the program could serve the community (Palmer, 1985). The investigation included a study of labor trends and requirements of agriculture-related occupations in the community. It found a demand for welders, small-engine mechanics, surveyors, grounds keepers, greenskeepers, florists, and agricultural sales and service employees. As a result, the district updated the program by adding courses in renewable natural resources, horticulture, and agricultural mechanics. It also hired an instructor to work with disadvantaged and handicapped students. Students now have opportunities for supervised occupational experiences in the school-run greenhouse, agricultural shop, orchard, landscape nursery, grounds, and livestock barns. They also participate in a cooperative work experience off campus during their junior and senior years (Palmer, 1985).

In Illinois, the Sycamore High School vocational agriculture program has likewise adapted to change. The traditional production agriculture program has been expanded, and new programs have been added in areas such as horticulture, landscaping, and greenhouse and nursery management (Guilinger and Dietz, 1985). Students may also enroll in courses in agriculture-related occupations, which combine on-the-job experience with course work.

The Anderson Valley Agricultural Institute (AVAI) of the Anderson Valley High School in Boonville, California, serves the needs of the entire student body, including high-risk and special-needs youth. Many of the high-risk and special-needs students live in local group homes and are enrolled in the vocational agriculture program for only a year or two. Program goals include reorienting these students, building their self-esteem, and creating an interest in agriculture and a desire to be in school. It is estimated that this program keeps as many as 10 of the 75 students enrolled in AVAI from dropping out of high school. In fact, many are motivated to go to college.

Student participation in the program is a better indicator of the program's success than job placement. The student population is transient because of the students in group homes. Students are sometimes allowed to return to their home schools before graduating from Anderson Valley. These factors lower the rate of program completion and job placement upon leaving the program (S. A. McKay, Anderson Valley High School, personal communication, 1988).

- **Federal and state education leaders should support the establishment of specialized secondary schools in each of three areas—urban, suburban, and rural. These schools should offer traditional academic courses that incorporate relevant agricultural topics to nurture agricultural literacy. They should also offer special courses in the agricultural sciences, nutrition, horticulture, agribusiness marketing and management, and other related agricultural subjects. Special federal and state financial incentives may be needed to help school districts establish such schools.**

Educational Technology

The science, technology, and business of agriculture are growing rapidly in complexity. Management and marketing decisions depend on access to a range of information and the capacity to apply it to appropriate circumstances.

As a first step, vocational agriculture classes, like others, should help prepare students to use computers as analytical and reference tools. Computers, video, and telecommunications can add new dimensions to vocational agriculture programs. These technologies can help teachers respond to student needs and interests as enrollment patterns and subject contents diversify. Moreover, initial investments made in hardware and software could reduce the costs of bringing new instructional modules and sources of information into vocational programs.

During its field visits, the committee learned about the use of computers and other forms of educational technology in some vocational agriculture programs. Although the use of electronic educational technology in these programs is limited, promising results have occurred in some applications.

The Ag Ed Network is one example of what can be accomplished with available technology. Part of the AgriData Network, the Ag Ed Network is used as a "live textbook" in many vocational agriculture classrooms. It provides news reports about agriculture; other forms of online information, particularly information dealing with agribusiness and marketing; and guidance on where more in-depth information can be obtained (B. Herz, AgriData Resources, Inc., personal communication, 1988). The committee found that vocational agriculture teachers who used or were familiar with the Ag Ed Network responded positively to it.

There has been insufficient time and experience with applications of new educational technologies in the vocational agriculture classroom to judge their full potential or the needs of teachers in adapting them to ongoing programs. It is not surprising that most of the vocational computer programs developed so far are oriented toward production agriculture. Some of these programs are useful in helping students to manage flocks and plan and track budgets. Software and other material on most nontraditional subjects are very limited. This scarcity is regrettable because the committee views such applications as among the most valuable and needed educational technologies.

Soon applications of biotechnology, including disease monitoring kits and other assay methods based on monoclonal antibodies, will be more accessible. Students will need to understand how these assay systems work and the conditions under which they are accurate. Interactive video discs can be used in conjunction with standard computers and software to guide students through specialized classroom projects and exercises. Advancing telecommunications or satellite technology will provide opportunities not widely available today in future classrooms. This technology could be very important to improving food and fiber literacy in the United States and other countries, as well as showing how agricultural and environmental concerns are closely linked.

- **Agriculture education teachers should seek out and share high-quality software and curricular materials for agriculture management and planning and instructional applications. Private-sector assistance should be sought in developing new instructional modules, exercises, and software.**
- **Political and business leaders at all levels should help teachers obtain access to promising instructional technologies. This help should include adequate funds to support use by teachers and students and troubleshooting assistance.**
- **Science curriculum development programs funded by fed-**

eral or state governments or private foundations and led by professional associations should pursue opportunities to use computers, video discs, and other educational technologies.

SUPERVISED OCCUPATIONAL EXPERIENCES

The supervised occupational experience (SOE) has long been a part of vocational agriculture and still is today. The committee identified several findings about the SOE component of vocational agricultural programs, including why it must adapt to future needs.

Testimony presented to the committee reinforced several common characteristics of high-quality SOEs. First, these SOEs were characterized by involved teachers, planned experiences, adequate resources, and student placement in agribusinesses or on commercial farms. A positive relationship typically exists between high-quality SOE programs and student achievement in vocational agriculture and employment in agriculture after graduation (Mick, 1983).

Second, in the committee's judgment, not all vocational agriculture students need SOEs throughout their 4-year vocational programs. Four years of SOE should remain the goal, however. In reality, some students may not have a meaningful SOE opportunity in all 4 years of program enrollment. Structural changes in agriculture have reduced the number and diversity of SOE opportunities in many areas. If teachers spend less time trying to develop SOEs where no great opportunities exist, they will have more time for other activities, including management of those students with SOEs. A student who wants to carry out a continuous 4-year SOE, such as an animal husbandry project, should not be discouraged or penalized for doing so. It is preferable to seek out and plan for 2 or 3 years of a rewarding SOE than to insist on a 4-year program of uneven quality or minimal relevance.

The growing importance of the food processing and marketing industries and the emergence of new jobs involving applications of biotechnology to agriculture may open up many new SOE opportunities in urban and rural communities. There are also many public service professionals who could become SOE sponsors. For example, a valuable SOE for a student could mean working as an elementary school teacher's aide and helping with a lesson plan in plant genetics, or with a nutritionist advising new mothers on how to care for infants in the areas of diet, nutrition, and health.

• **As a goal, all students should participate in worthwhile SOEs while enrolled in vocational agriculture programs. Students should not be penalized in their program standing or**

FFA activities if a suitable high-quality SOE is sometimes unavailable.

• A broader range of SOEs should be encouraged. SOEs should include time in research laboratories, banks, and food retailing and marketing and work with commodity markets, elementary schools, and many other new areas. Cooperation and commitment should be sought from the agribusiness community. Emphasis should be placed on the experience and entrepreneurship, not only on the occupation.

• Special summer SOE programs should be explored as an alternative in school districts where students cannot locate high-quality SOE opportunities. Summer programs might even involve travel to locations where desirable SOEs are available. Some locations might include an agricultural experiment station, a food processing factory, or an industrial laboratory.

• Although management and financial skills should be a part of most production-oriented SOEs, profit should only occasionally be a principal factor in evaluating SOE achievements. Public service and academic endeavors, such as work in an elementary classroom or a research laboratory, respectively, should be encouraged. The emphasis of SOEs should be on learning, with an appreciation for earning.

• Schools should consider providing on-site laboratory facilities for SOEs that involve activities that can be undertaken after school without interfering with other instructional programs. School land laboratories, greenhouses, nurseries, grounds, and agricultural mechanics laboratories can provide opportunities.

FUTURE FARMERS OF AMERICA

As a national organization, the FFA has been part of vocational agriculture since 1928. The FFA is dedicated to fostering leadership, self-confidence, and citizenship skills. It also strives to teach students to appreciate agriculture and about the career opportunities open to them in the agriculture and food and fiber industries. About 95 percent of all secondary schools that offer vocational agriculture have an FFA chapter, and about 75 percent of vocational agriculture students are members (National FFA Organization, 1986).

Under the direction of the vocational agriculture teacher, FFA members hold meetings, practice public speaking, demonstrate proficiency in various occupational skills, participate in community improvement efforts, and earn awards through local, state, and national contests. It is clear that students in high-quality FFA chapters gain far more from the program than those in lower-quality FFA chapters.

The quality of FFA chapters varies as much as the quality of vocational agriculture programs varies. As an organization for high school students enrolled in vocational agriculture, the FFA has a record of accomplishment and the capacity to foster individual improvement. For many students, the FFA achieves its goal of developing entrepreneurial skills, leadership, and citizenship. Still, the FFA's image, name, symbols, ceremonies, and production-agriculture focus lessen for many students the attractiveness of enrollment in vocational agriculture programs and interfere with needed changes in the curriculum content of these programs.

The committee believes the FFA needs to change its image. The organization must broaden its nearly exclusive focus on traditional production agriculture. Even its name, the Future Farmers of America, continues to reinforce a narrow view of the organization, vocational agriculture education, and agriculture in general. Although some people have suggested that dropping the "Future Farmers of America" name and only using the FFA initials would change the FFA's image, it is doubtful. To the public, the full name and the initials are well known and interchangeable.

Based on evidence and testimony, the committee finds that some vocational agriculture teachers are unduly driven by a desire to help students excel in traditional production-oriented FFA contests and award programs. These teachers tend to place less emphasis on delivering agricultural instruction in the classroom, updating curricula, or involving the business community in the vocational agriculture program. In many communities, the high school vocational agriculture program is known as the "FFA program"; the vocational agriculture teacher is known as the "FFA teacher." In such schools, it is hard to direct public attention toward the need for curriculum reform or agriculture's role in college preparation or more career opportunities. In many vocational programs a principal focus of class time and extracurricular activity is preparing students to compete in traditional, production-oriented FFA contests and award programs.

The committee recognizes that the FFA may be slow to change or disagree about the need or direction for change. The committee is hopeful, though, that the FFA's ongoing reviews of its name, traditions, procedures, contests, awards, and degree requirements for advancement will lead to constructive changes. The FFA is also supporting efforts to develop new science-based instructional materials and special activities to foster understanding of scientific and technological developments important to the agricultural, food, and fiber industries.

For example, the FFA has a program that recognizes vocational agriculture teachers who have shown that they use applied agricultural science effectively in their instruction and students who have demonstrated the use of agricultural science principles in their research projects. Similar FFA activities are needed that accompany curriculum development projects in the marketing, management, policy, financial, and international aspects of agriculture.

• **In high schools that have vocational agriculture programs but do not have FFA chapters, the FFA should explore ways to make the organization accessible.**

• **The FFA should adopt a new name, symbols, and rituals (according to all applicable federal and state laws) consistent with a contemporary, forward-looking image of agriculture.**

• **The FFA should revise the nature, focus, and award struc-**

PHOTOGRAPH: NATIONAL FFA ORGANIZATION

Many students become interested in chemistry and biology through exposure to examples from the agricultural sciences. Here, a student at Canby Union High School, Canby, Oregon, completes a soil test to determine soil fertility.

PHOTOGRAPH: NATIONAL FFA ORGANIZATION

Steven A. McKay of Anderson Valley High School, Boonville, California, assists two of his students to clone a plant using tissue culture technology. McKay interests his students in science by involving them in cloning plants, testing new horticultural products, and engineering better ways to grow food.

ture of its contests and activities to open more new categories of competition in areas outside production agriculture; reduce the number of production-oriented activities and programs; attract minorities and girls into vocational agriculture programs; and minimize absences and conflicts with regular school programs.

• The FFA should encourage enrollment by students unable or unwilling to participate in a 4-year program of vocational agriculture or SOEs.

TEACHER EDUCATION

Vocational agriculture relies on dedicated teachers. The committee is concerned that vocational agriculture teachers are still being prepared to teach mainly traditional production agriculture. To offer more current programs to a broader range of students, teachers will need to acquire knowledge and teaching skills related to agribusiness marketing, public policy, economics, finance, science and technology, and international agriculture.

In the United States, vocational agriculture teachers are educated in 89 programs in colleges and universities. For the Peters and Moore (1984) study, survey recipients in only 64 programs responded. Of that number, 69 percent are based in schools of agriculture, and 31 percent in colleges of education. In some states, teachers may enter the field without degrees on the basis of occupational experience alone. Other states require competency tests (W. G. Camp, Virginia Polytechnic Institute and State University, personal communication, 1988).

Vocational agriculture teacher education combines instruction about agriculture with instruction in teaching. Recently, greater emphasis has been placed on communication skills, basic science, computers, mathematics, humanities and social sciences, international agricultural systems, problem-based instruction, and high-technology agriculture. The emphasis on traditional production agriculture is beginning to shift, albeit slowly (Reisch, 1986).

Graduates who accepted positions as vocational agriculture teachers reported that the practical and technical parts of their schooling were the most useful, while courses in education, pedagogy, and the humanities were the least useful. Other studies found that vocational agriculture teachers identified student teaching as the most helpful part of their education (Lee, 1985).

The number of agriculture education graduates qualified to teach dropped from 1,207 in 1985 to 964 in 1986. This decline resulted in the smallest number of graduates since 1965. The decline is also accelerating. Between 1975 and 1980, the number dropped 5 percent; between 1980 and 1985, 24 percent (Camp, 1987).

Only a portion of graduates enters teaching (Camp, 1987). In 1965, 64.6 percent of newly qualified teachers of agriculture education entered teaching. In 1986, the percentage had fallen to 41.2 percent (Camp, 1987). The same study found that the proportion of agriculture education graduates who entered agribusiness rose from 7.5 percent in 1975 to 16.3 percent in 1986.

At the same time, fewer vocational agriculture teaching jobs exist. In 1986, there were 11,042 positions in the United States. This figure continues the general downward trend that began in 1979, following a 1978 peak of 12,844 (Camp, 1987). The decline from 1985 to 1986 has been the largest of the 1980s, resulting in 5 percent, or 645, fewer positions (Camp, 1987).

Declining enrollments continue to reduce the number of vocational agriculture teaching jobs. The number of vocational agriculture departments that could not operate in the fall of 1986 because of the lack of a qualified teacher fell for the first time to zero (Camp, 1987). The committee is skeptical, however, that there is an adequate supply of teachers with the broader range of interests and teaching skills that may be needed in future agriculture courses of the type recommended in this report.

• **Teacher education programs in agriculture should continue to stress applied learning, but should strengthen instruction in science, technology, economics, agribusiness marketing and management, international agriculture, and public policy.**

• **The federal government and elementary and secondary school teachers involved in teaching agriculture should work to develop, refine, and adopt methods for the transfer of information and knowledge from research laboratories and agricultural experiment stations to high school classrooms. An emphasis is needed on new methods to teach agribusiness marketing and management, principles of science, public policy, and international agriculture.**

• **Teacher education programs in agriculture should establish formal links with colleges of agriculture and education, cooperative extension, and private-sector organizations to develop new in-service programs and opportunities for teachers and administrators.**

• **Colleges of agriculture should become more involved in curriculum reform, creation of new material and courses, and in-service education programs. The USDA should encourage these goals. One way to do this might be to provide challenge grants to states seeking to create new linkages between agricultural education administrators and faculty within colleges of agriculture and education. Each state should examine the feasibility of developing a center for curriculum design and teacher and administrators counselor training based at its land-grant university.**

• **Teacher educators in agriculture should establish better links with colleagues in other colleges, such as experts in science education, business management, and educational technology.**

• **Colleges of agriculture should encourage and help recruit talented students to enter the teaching profession. Departments of agriculture education should develop programs to inform school district counselors about career opportunities in the agricultural education professions.**

Text
References

AGFOCUS: A Project of America's Governors, Inc. 1986. An Analysis of Contemporary Attitudes on Some Basic Issues. Helena, Mont.: AGFOCUS. 44 pp.

Bowen, Homer. Testimony before Committee on Agricultural Education in Secondary Schools, May 12, 1986. California State Polytechnic University, Pomona, Calif.

Camp, W. G. 1986. A National Study of the Supply and Demand for Teachers of Vocational Agriculture in 1985. Blacksburg, Va.: Division of Vocational and Technical Education, Virginia Polytechnic Institute and State University.

Camp, W. G. 1987. A National Study of the Supply and Demand for Teachers of Vocational Agriculture in 1986. Blacksburg, Va.: Division of Vocational and Technical Education, Virginia Polytechnic Institute and State University.

Coulter, K. J., M. Stanton, and A. D. Goecker. 1986. Employment Opportunities for College Graduates in the Food and Agricultural Sciences. Washington, D.C.: U.S. Department of Agriculture.

Darrow, E. D., ed. 1985. The Science Workbook of Student Research Projects in Food–Agriculture–Natural Resources. Columbus, Ohio: College of Agriculture, Ohio State University.

Feltham, W. 1986. Life lab: a community-based elementary science program. California Science Teacher's Journal 16(2):18–25.

Garner-Koech, B. 1985. Teacher Resource Book: Grades 4–6. Amherst, Mass: Massachusetts Agriculture in the Classroom, Inc.

Guilinger, J., and A. Dietz. 1985. 1985 Annual Report: Sycamore Vocational Agriculture Department. Sycamore, Ill.: Sycamore High School.

Hart, C. W. 1985. 'Learning to do, doing to learn' at Saul School. Chestnut Hill Local, 29 August 1985.

Heath, R. L. Testimony before Committee on Agricultural Education in Secondary Schools, May 13–14, 1986. California State Polytechnic University, Pomona, Calif.

Higgins, C. M. A. 1984. A Study to Determine Attitudes and Practices of West Virginia Vocational Agriculture Teachers Toward Enrollment of Female Students. West Virginia University, Morgantown. Master's degree thesis.

Horn, J., and B. Vining. 1986. An Assessment of Students' Knowledge of Agriculture. Manhattan, Kans.: Center of Extended Services and Studies, College of Education, Kansas State University.

Jaffe, R., M. Cadoux, and G. Appel, eds. 1985. The Growing Classroom. Capitola, Calif.: Friends of the Harvest, Life Lab Science Programs. 3 vols.

Lee, J. S., ed. 1985. Agricultural Education: Review and Synthesis of the Research, Fourth Ed. Information Series No. 298. Columbus, Ohio: ERIC Clearinghouse on Adult, Career, and Vocational Education. The National Center for Research in Vocational Education,

Lee, J. S. 1986. Vocational agriculture teacher preparation. Pp. 95–100 in Technology, the Economy, and Vocational Education. S. A. Rosenfeld, ed. Research Triangle Park, N.C.: Southern Growth Policies Board.

Leising, J. G., and K. Emo. 1984. Gender Equity: California Future Farmers of America. Staff Study. Davis, Calif.: University of California.

Life Lab Science Program. 1988. Life Lab awarded $2.1 million. Capitola, Calif.: Life Lab Science Program. 1 p.

Mallory, M. E., and R. Sommer. 1986a. Student images of agriculture: survey highlights and recommendations. Journal of the American Association of Teacher Educators in Agriculture 27(4):15, 24–25.

Mallory, M. E., and R. Sommer. 1986b. Students show low awareness of agricultural careers. California Agriculture March/April 1986:4–6.

McClay, D. R. 1978. Identifying and Validating Essential Competencies Needed for Entry and Advancement in Major Agricultural and Agribusiness Occupations. Final Report. ERIC Document Reproduction Service No. ED 151 521. State College, Pa.: Instructional Consulting and Research Associates, Inc.

Mick, J. H. 1983. Relationships Between Agricultural Background and Job Placement of Vo-Ag Graduates in Missouri. Ph.D. dissertation. University of Missouri, Columbia.

Moore, J. A. 1987. New wine in old bottles? The Agricultural Education Magazine 60(4):5–6.

National Academies of Sciences and Engineering. 1982. Science and Mathematics in the Schools: Report of a Convocation. Washington, D.C.: National Academy Press.

National FFA (Future Farmers of America) Organization. 1986. Participation in Selected FFA Activities. Alexandria, Va.: National FFA (Future Farmers of America) Organization.

National Science Resources Center. 1986. Report on the NSRC National Conference on the Teaching of Science in Elementary Schools. Washington, D.C.: National Science Resources Center. 3 pp.

Oliver, J. D. 1986. Vocational agriculture education's response to the educational reform movement. Paper presented at Southern Regional Agricultural Education Conference, Little Rock, Ark., March 24, 1986.

Otto, J. H., and A. Towle. 1985. Modern Biology. New York: Holt, Rinehart and Winston.

Palmer, W. H. 1985. Vocational Agriculture Past, Present and Future. Paper Presented to: Committee on Agricultural Education in Secondary Schools, National Research Council, National Academy of Sciences. Alvirne High School, Hudson, N.H. October 22. Photocopy.

Parmley, J. D. 1982. The Need for Vocational Agriculture Instruction in Kansas

Counties Where Such Instruction Does Not Exist. Staff study. Manhattan, Kans.: Kansas State University.

Parmley, J. D., R. F. Welton, and M. Bender. 1981. Opinions of Agriculture Teachers, School Administrators, Students and Parents Concerning Females as Agriculture Students, Teachers and Workers in Agriculture. ERIC Document Reproduction Service No. ED 209 488. Manhattan, Kans.: Department of Adult and Occupational Education, Kansas State University.

Peters, J., and G. Moore. 1984. A comparison of agricultural education programs located in colleges of agriculture with those located in colleges of education. Journal of the American Association of Teacher Educators in Agriculture 25(3):29–38.

Petrulis, M., B. L. Green, F. Hines, R. Nolan, and J. Sommer. 1987. How Is Farm Financial Stress Affecting Rural America? Agricultural Economic Report No. 568. Washington, D.C.: Economic Research Service, USDA.

Reisch, Kenneth W. 1986. Testimony before Committee on Agricultural Education in Secondary Schools, May 12, 1986. California State Polytechnic University, Pomona, Calif.

Roberts, R. W. 1971. Vocational and Practical Arts Education. New York: Harper & Row.

Russell, E. S. 1987. A model for instruction in agrisciences and agribusiness. The Agricultural Education Magazine 60(4):7–8.

Standards for Quality Vocational Programs in Agricultural/Agribusiness Education. 1977. Ames, Iowa: Department of Agricultural Education, Iowa State University.

U.S. Commission on Civil Rights. 1982. The Decline of Black Farming in America. Washington, D.C.: U.S. Government Printing Office.

U.S. Department of Agriculture (USDA). 1987. Science and Technology: The 4-H Way. Status Report: 1986. Extension Service, Cooperative Extension System. Washington, D.C.: U.S. Government Printing Office.

U.S. Department of Agriculture (USDA). 1988. State Updates: Ag in the Classroom. Washington, D.C.: U.S. Department of Agriculture.

U.S. Department of Commerce Bureau of the Census. 1988. Statistical Abstract of the United States: 1988., 108th Ed. Washington, D.C.: U.S. Government Printing Office.

U.S. Department of Education (USDE) Center for Education Statistics. 1983. The Condition of Education, 1983 Ed., V. W. Plisko, ed. Washington, D.C.: U.S. Government Printing Office.

U.S. Department of Education (USDE) Center for Education Statistics. 1987. The Condition of Education, 1987 Ed., J. D. Stern and M. O. Chandler, eds. Washington, D.C.: U.S. Government Printing Office.

U.S. Departments of Agriculture and Commerce. 1986. Farm Population of the United States, 1985. Washington, D.C.: U.S. Government Printing Office.

Walter Biddle Saul High School of Agricultural Sciences. 1980. Academic and General Programs of Study in Preparation for College or Vocational Pursuits. Philadelphia, Pa.: Walter Biddle Saul High School of Agricultural Sciences. 8 pp.

Walter Biddle Saul High School of Agricultural Sciences. 1984. Agricultural curriculum and subject selection. Walter Biddle Saul High School of Agricultural Sciences, Philadelphia, Pa. December 6. Photocopy.

Walter Biddle Saul High School of Agricultural Sciences. N.d. Fox Chase Farm. Philadelphia, Pa.: Walter Biddle Saul High School of Agricultural Sciences. 1 p.

Weiss, I. R. 1987. Report of the 1985–1986 National Survey of Science and Mathematics Education. Research Triangle Park, N.C.: Research Triangle Institute.

The Changing Face of American Agriculture

Nearly 400 years ago, colonists began to settle and clear the eastern seaboard of what would become the United States. The settlers transformed forests into crop land and pasture. They planted some seeds native to the new land and some they had brought from their homelands. They gradually built into herds the domesticated animals they brought with them. Farms grew, prospered, and multiplied.

Over time, farming methods became more sophisticated, and yields and the area of land under cultivation increased. Farmers became more knowledgeable about which crop plants and animals were suitable for the highly varied climates and conditions around the United States.

This growth notwithstanding, farms were largely self-contained enterprises until about the 1930s, when the agricultural sciences began to progress rapidly. A scientific and technological revolution swept American agriculture as hybrid seeds, synthetic fertilizers, pesticides, and sophisticated machinery became available. Farmers came to rely on others for information, services, and important production inputs such as fertilizers and crop protection chemicals. Much of the new technology was labor-saving, which helped to increase growth in farm size. This new technology also made manpower more available during the war years and for industrial development.

Today, farmers purchase most of their basic production inputs from off the farm. Labor, management, replacement livestock, and farm-grown feed for livestock are the major inputs that still are often largely derived from or provided on the farm. Machinery, seeds, fertilizers, pesticides, livestock breeding stock, and capital are acquired off the farm, and must be paid for from annual farm earnings.

The demise of the self-contained farm has made farming a complex, even more risky way of life. Most farmers have to borrow money each year to help finance the high annual costs of producing and harvesting a crop, while complying with a wide range of government program rules and regulatory standards.

Shrinking markets, greater global competition, fluctuating land values, and declining prices for commodities in the 1980s placed many farmers in serious financial difficulties. Many have moved out of farming. The farm crisis that began in 1981 is not over. The adjustments that American agriculture must make to remain competitive will affect agriculture's major supporting institutions and programs, including agricultural education.

STRUCTURAL AND POLICY CHANGES

Technological and economic forces have led to a reduction in the number of farms and a comparable increase in average farm size. In the 1930s, there were 6.3 million farms in the United States. Today, about 2.3 million remain. Farmers made up 30 percent of the U.S. population in 1920 and 15 percent in 1950. In 1985, only 2.2 percent of Americans lived on farms—and only half of all employed farm residents reported agriculture as their main occupation. Nevertheless, nearly 20 percent of the labor force works for the agricultural industry in some capacity (Petrulis et al., 1987). Very large farms now dominate the farm economy. Today, about 1 percent of U.S. farms account for nearly two-thirds of net cash farm income (USDA Economic Research Service, 1985; U.S. Department of Commerce Bureau of the Census and USDA Economic Research Service, 1986).

Agricultural policies through the last few decades have also influenced the structure of agriculture by influencing the types and sizes of farms that can most effectively earn profits. Commodity programs have encouraged farmers to specialize in the production of one crop or a few related ones. They have also provided unintended incentives to farmers to use fragile soil and water resources for crop production. For decades, the programs have rewarded farmers for increasing the number of acres they can enroll in farm programs and for using fertilizers and pesticides to increase average yields as much as possible. Yet, the basic purpose of the programs has been to increase farm income by holding back production levels in relation to demand.

Agricultural research and extension education programs responded to the needs of farmers seeking greater efficiency, higher yields, and more specialization. Vocational agriculture programs also followed suit, focusing in different parts of the country on changing crops, enterprises, and production methods.

The integration of the American agricultural sector into the international economy advanced in the 1970s, as the United States continued to export products and production expertise around the world. Since 1980, however, international recession, declining world dependence on food exports, and increased competition for agricultural export markets have affected U.S. agricultural trade adversely. Marketing, finance, and trading skills needed to regain markets are becoming more dominant factors in successful agribusinesses. These factors are also setting new priorities for business persons, policymakers, financiers, and educators, including agricultural educators.

Scientific progress is continuing to generate new techniques to increase crop yields; improve livestock health, reproduction, and growth; and develop new strategies to reduce production costs. Biotechnology and information technology have the potential—already realized in some cases—to improve agricultural productivity and fundamentally alter the characteristics of food and fiber products and production processes (NRC, 1985; OTA, 1986; NRC, 1987a,b). Animal production is likely to be the first area at the farm level to benefit markedly from biotechnology in the next decade, with plant production following toward the end of the century (OTA, 1986).

Embryo transfers, gene insertion, growth hormones, and other technologies stemming from genetic engineering will result in dairy cows that produce more milk while consuming less feed and livestock that grow faster with fewer pounds of feed. By the end of this century, biotechnology will allow some major crops to be altered genetically so that they become naturally resistant to the diseases and insects that now force farmers to treat crops with pesticides. Other developments will make possible crops with the ability to produce a higher level or quality of protein, manufacture their own plant nutrients, and suppress weeds and insects.

Increasing international competition in food and fiber markets—including the U.S. food market—will force U.S. farmers and agribusinesses to adapt and keep pace with technological advances and market opportunities. Leaders in American agriculture stress the need to develop management skills to use new technologies more effectively. Leaders also see a need for policy reform if U.S. agriculture is to compete profitably in international markets. Even more so than in the past, human skills, creativity, and knowledge will be fundamental to building and sustaining U.S. agriculture's competitive edge. Hence, the role of agricultural education today is more important than ever for the professional in agriculture as well as the consumer, policymaker, and business person.

APPENDIX

B

Agricultural Education
in America

$\mathbf{A}$griculture was first taught formally in the United States in Georgia in 1733. There, colonists were trying to learn native methods of cultivation and identify the crops and techniques best suited to their new home. In 1734, the Salzburger family established what was probably the first specialized school of agriculture—an orphans' school in Ebenezer, Georgia, where children were taught to farm successfully (Moore, 1987).

In the first half of the nineteenth century, some schools offered instruction in agriculture. But as was true for most practical skills, agriculture was taught principally by parents, who passed along to their children the skills and knowledge they needed to take over the family farm or manage their own farm.

The passage of the Morrill Act in 1862 set the stage for more formal agricultural education. This act reflected the importance that policymakers placed on agriculture. It provided for the support and maintenance of state colleges where citizens could be taught agricultural and mechanical arts (Tenney, 1977).

Early public support for agricultural education varied in format. In 1862, Massachusetts became the first state to enact legislation encouraging agricultural instruction, while Tennessee became the first to require it in 1891. Connecticut was the first state to provide funds for state schools of agriculture in 1881, followed by Rhode Island in 1888 and New Hampshire in 1895. Alabama provided funds for regional schools of agriculture in 1897. In 1901, Wisconsin became the first state to provide funds for county agricultural high schools or independent

54

agricultural schools. And it was Virginia, in 1908, that first funded agricultural departments in public schools (Warmbrod, 1962).

Throughout these years the campaign for agricultural instruction was local and rural. The efforts of the Grange in the 1860s represented the first organized, political attempt to create what is known today as agricultural literacy (Cremin, 1961).

Agricultural education in the nineteenth century differed significantly from other occupational education in content and approach. An emphasis on science characterized most programs. Rural educators viewed instruction in science and nature as a way to make public education relevant to rural life.

The high school curriculum in many states included agronomy, laboratory and field work, rural engineering, and farm mechanics (Crosby, 1912). These early programs served two purposes: one related to the out-migration of youth to the cities, and the second to the need to provide new skills and learning potential to those children that remained on the farm (Rosenfeld, 1984).

The federal government stepped into the picture in 1907, when the U.S. Congress passed the Nelson Amendments to the Morrill Act. These amendments provided the first federal funds to prepare teachers of agriculture. In effect, the amendments supplemented states' legislation by providing an institutional base for preparing teachers (Swanson, 1986).

During these years, vocational agriculture began to develop the philosophy and traditions that characterize it today. Agricultural education has always been much broader in scope than the occupational programs designed for business and other industries. In 1909 the U.S. Office of Experiment Stations published a paper on high school agricultural education, urging that "the standard agricultural courses, whether in ordinary high schools or in special schools, should not be narrowly vocational, but should aim to fit the pupils for life as progressive, broadminded, and intelligent men and women, citizens and homemakers, as well as farmers and horticulturalists" (True, 1929).

A 1911 analysis by F. W. Howe, an agriculture specialist with the New York Department of Education, describes some of the issues faced by educators in the early years of this century. They recognized that the nation's well-being depended in large part on a flourishing agricultural sector. But they were uncertain how instruction about agriculture—vocational or otherwise—should be integrated into general education; at what age such instruction should begin; and who should bear the cost (Howe, 1911). These questions remain very much on today's agenda.

THE EARLY GROWTH YEARS

A growing number of schools added agriculture to their curricula through the early 1900s. In 1900, about 400 high schools offered instruction in agriculture or its applications to botany, chemistry, or zoology. By 1912, 2,000 high schools offered such instruction. In 1915, this number had doubled, and 11 states appropriated funds specifically for agricultural education in high schools. A single teacher in each school was usually responsible for agricultural education. Most of those teachers had been employed to teach science (True, 1929).

By the 1915–1916 school year, 28 secondary schools of agriculture at state agricultural colleges, 124 public normal schools, and 74 special agricultural schools receiving state aid offered agricultural instruction. Four hundred twenty-one high schools under state supervision had vocational agriculture departments; about 2,600 public high schools that were not state funded offered agriculture. Twelve private agricultural secondary schools taught agriculture, as did 149 private secondary schools. In the racially segregated education system of the era, agriculture was also taught at 107 secondary and higher schools for black students (True, 1929).

In 1917, Congress further defined the federal role in agricultural education with the passage of the Smith-Hughes Act, which included specific provisions for agricultural education. The passage of this act marked the point at which "vocational agriculture" diverged from and largely replaced general agricultural education in the schools. The act established a federally funded vocational education program that included very specific provisions for agricultural education. Not all educators agreed with the shift toward a more vocational approach, and some schools did not adopt the new vocational agriculture programs.

The vocational agriculture programs that developed after the Smith-Hughes Act were intended to prepare young people to be or to work as farmers. The goal was to provide a curriculum more relevant to their needs than the academic programs used in city schools. But the programs did more than prepare farmers; they also helped to spread knowledge throughout farming regions about how and when to use agricultural innovations and which soil and animal husbandry practices might overcome longstanding problems.

With a distinctive mission, vocational agriculture developed an equally distinctive approach to instruction. Teachers of vocational agriculture sought to engage students in tasks that taught process and content. This was done through a mixture of classroom instruction, work experience, and entrepreneurship. Teachers encouraged students to make independent decisions and take initiative. Programs were designed so students could see directly how their newly acquired skills and knowledge improved production (Rosenfeld, 1984).

Typically, curricula covered a wide range of topics. The new vocational agriculture programs were not rural versions of the vocational trade and industrial education programs being established in the cities. Farming was not simply a job, but a way of life. The challenges of farming were as varied as the American landscape, and the hundreds of commodities and products that the landscape yielded. Nor was the farmer an employee who needed education in skills that subsequently would be used under the guidance of management in a structured work environment.

Farmers were independent business people and entrepreneurs who made and acted upon many decisions, and then lived with the consequences. To make these decisions intelligently, farmers needed to know much more than practical skills, such as plowing and planting. They needed analytical problem-solving skills to decide what to produce; how to use available land, labor, and other resources; and how to overcome adversity. They also needed to understand and apply scientific knowledge and experimental methods, financial analyses, and sound business practices.

Agricultural educators strove for three basic goals in their curricula and programs. They tried to be comprehensive in coverage, scientific in method, and practical in impact and focus. One important innovation to achieve this complex union of characteristics was the use of "supervised farming," which agricultural educator Rufus W. Stimson pioneered. Stimson first used this approach when he became director of the Smith Agricultural School in Northhampton, Massachusetts, in 1908 (Moore, 1985). The 1917 Smith-Hughes Act incorporated the method into vocational agriculture nationwide. The act contained a provision that "in order to receive the benefits of such appropriation, . . . such schools shall provide for directed or supervised practice in agriculture" (P.L. #64-347).

Another important development was the founding of the Future Farmers of America in 1928. The FFA grew out of the boys' and girls' clubs of the early 1900s and soon became an integral part of high school vocational agriculture for boys. By working closely with business and industry, the FFA provided many rural young people with an opportunity for economic, political, and civic leadership. The FFA also provided parents and other members of the community opportunities for involvement in a variety of educational and recreational activities directly linked to local farming and business activities.

The growth in the organization closely matched growth in enrollment in vocational agriculture programs. The FFA grew from 105 chapters in 18 states in 1928 to 8,577 chapters in the 50 states, Puerto Rico, and the Virgin Islands in 1986 (Tenney, 1977; National FFA Organization, 1986). Approximately 75 percent of students enrolled in vocational agriculture courses belong to the FFA, and approximately 95 percent of vocational agricultural departments sponsor an FFA chapter (see Chapter 3 for further details on vocational agriculture and FFA enrollment trends).

After vocational agriculture was incorporated into vocational education, changes followed quickly (Warmbrod, 1962). For example, David Snedden, one of the period's leading vocational educators, criticized vocational agriculture for not providing a sufficiently specialized education (Snedden, 1918). Citing the contemporary corporation as his model, Snedden urged agriculture educators to narrow the breadth of their curricula and teach farmers to rely more on experts for information and decisions.

Despite these pressures to become more like industrial education, vocational agriculture, with its own support system in rural communities and the agricultural industry, retained its distinctive identity among federal vocational education programs. Gradually, however, changing attitudes toward vocational education affected it. College became much more accessible, and schools' curricula reflected the need to prepare students for advanced education. College-bound and vocational students began following different educational paths. By tracking college-bound and vocational students after graduation, educators learned more about the types of students who pursued the two paths, and the types of jobs the students took after graduation. As a result, science and academic skills came to be considered preparation for college and assumed a lower priority in vocational agriculture (Rosenfeld, 1984).

In 1963, Congress enacted a new vocational education law that reshaped vocational agriculture and altered its relationship to other vocational programs (P.L. #88-210).

Four elements of this law proved particularly significant. First, it aimed federal vocational education funds to meet labor market demand and replaced funds earmarked for specific occupational areas with one block grant. The practical results of this were that vocational agriculture had to compete for funds with seven other occupational areas, and labor market projections came to drive state funding allocations. Second, the regulations promulgated under the new law divided vocational agriculture into areas of specialization. Agriculture teachers had to classify students by specialized agricultural codes and measure program success by students' employment in specialized areas after graduation. Third, the new law placed greater emphasis on persons with special needs, such as the handicapped or disadvantaged students. Finally, the new law officially broadened the purpose of vocational agriculture to include "off-farm" agriculture. At this point, the term supervised farming was changed to the still-current "supervised occupational experience," a term that encompasses a far broader range of activities, including construction, secretarial work, and agricultural research (Crawford and Cooper, 1986).

Later changes in federal legislation have placed further emphasis on the special needs of women, members of minority groups, and handicapped and disadvantaged students. The Carl D. Perkins Act, approved by Congress in 1984, mitigates some of the effects of the 1963 law by expanding the measures of success to include "basic employment competencies" instead of employment alone (P.L. #98-524). These competencies include many of the strengths on which vocational agriculture is based: basic problem-solving skills, entrepreneurial development and attitudes, and practical applications of scientific concepts and experimental methods.

The Education Reform Movement of the 1980s

$\mathbf{I}$n the 1980s, a crusade to improve public education gathered momentum. The movement began as several states sought to correct long-standing problems in public schools.

In 1983, the education reform movement gained national prominence with the publication of the report, *A Nation at Risk* (National Commission on Excellence in Education, 1983). That report criticized American education and issued several recommendations to remedy perceived problems. The commission recommended 4 years of English, 3 years of mathematics, 3 years of science, 3 years of social studies, and one-half year of computer science for high school students seeking a diploma. The commission strongly recommended 2 years of foreign language for college-bound students. The report suggested that the school day be lengthened or students spend more of the year in school, and schools renew their commitment to basic skills and academic subjects.

A Nation at Risk spurred action at all levels of government. Governors and state legislatures that had not already done so began to create panels and develop strategies for educational reform. In some cases, individual school boards began reform plans of their own (USDE, 1984).

The education reform movement touches virtually all aspects of education. Its general theme, however, is that more should be demanded of teachers, students, and administrators, and basic subjects and cognitive skills should be reemphasized.

One set of reforms sought to improve the quality and skills of teachers. It was found that as a group, college students who planned to major in education had low scores on Scholastic Aptitude Tests (The College Board, 1985). To remedy this problem, schools and colleges of teacher education are focusing on recruitment to attract and retain better students and upgrading course work contents and requirements for prospective teachers (USDE, 1984).

Reformers also criticized the required curricula for undergraduate and graduate degrees in education, which, they argued, showed future teachers how to teach but not what to teach. Because teacher certification in most states requires some credits in education, college graduates with biology or English degrees who subsequently decide upon a teaching career have to return to school to take required education courses. Critics argued that such requirements keep many highly skilled individuals out of the classroom. To encourage these people to pursue careers in teaching, a few states have developed teacher preparation programs for graduates with liberal arts and science degrees. The programs generally involve participation in a 1-year or short-term intensive teacher education program that grants full certification to those who complete it.

Testing of the skills and knowledge of teacher candidates also became more common in the early 1980s, following reports that documented deficiencies among active teachers. The National Teacher Examination became more widely used for individuals first entering the teaching profession. Some states also began testing teachers already at work.

The education reform movement affected teachers already in the classroom in other ways, too. Following the lead of Tennessee's then-Governor Lamar Alexander, states and school districts began trying to assemble "master teacher" or "career ladder" plans. The goals of these plans were to reward excellent teachers with higher status and more money, as well as to use these teachers as mentors and models for less experienced colleagues. In practice, however, the plans proved very difficult to set up; objective criteria for "excellence" were not easily defined. Nevertheless, the career ladder concept is still being tried in some places.

Most of the recommendations that came out of the reform movement were aimed at students. The quality and the quantity of instruction were generally found wanting.

In the area of quality, reformers criticized the emphasis on instruction that did not demand that students think critically and analytically. Results of the National Assessment for Educational Progress (NAEP) found that students had improved in basic skills in recent years and could now read and perform simple arithmetic better than students could a decade earlier. But when confronted with questions that demanded analysis or critical thinking, students did not improve. They were not adequately taught to solve problems, only to recognize correct answers (NAEP, 1982).

Education in mathematics, science, and foreign languages was found

particularly deficient. A 1980 report by the NSF and USDE characterized Americans as "scientific illiterates." It found that students received too little instruction in science and mathematics to prepare them
for their roles as workers and citizens in a highly technological society
(NSF and USDE, 1980). In 1983, a commission appointed by the National Science Board (NSB) proposed a plan to remedy the deficiencies
in mathematics and science instruction (NSB Commission on Precollege Education in Mathematics, Science, and Technology, 1983). The
commission recommended that substantial science instruction begin
in the early years of school and be integrated into the curriculum in a
way that gives students more hands-on experience. As students progress through school, instruction should continue to illuminate the
links between science, society, and practical problems such as energy
use, pollution, and disease.

Most education officials and policymakers responded to these criti-
cisms in a straightforward way: they raised graduation requirements.
Many state colleges and land grant universities imposed stricter entrance requirements, typically involving more academic credits. In
many states where students were required to take one science course
before receiving a diploma, they are now required to take two or three.
The same is true for mathematics and, in some cases, foreign
languages.

Increasing requirements for the number of hours devoted to these
basic academic courses soon raised new concerns. Time available for
electives and extracurricular activities was reduced, as were opportunities to explore different subjects or take vocational courses. Nor was
it enough simply to require more of the same abstract science typically
offered—what students needed to learn was how science and technology affect the world. Some agricultural educators were already working to incorporate more science into vocational agriculture courses, but
they found it harder to attract students who had to fit more academic
subjects into their school day.

The long-term effects of the educational reform movement on electives are still not known. Whether vocational agriculture will flourish
under the new requirements will depend at least in part on its own
capacity to be flexible and scientifically rigorous. Vocational agriculture can achieve this rigor by satisfying, in part, newly imposed graduation and college entrance requirements.

Appendix
References

The College Board. 1985. National College-Bound Seniors, 1985. Princeton, N.J.: The College Board.

Crawford, D. S., and E. L. Cooper. 1986. The impact of the vocational education act of 1963 on agricultural education. Paper presented at the National Agricultural Education Research Meeting, Dallas, December 5, 1986.

Cremin, L. J. 1961. The Transformation of the School. New York: Vintage.

Crosby, D. J. 1912. Agriculture in public high schools. In Yearbook of the Department of Agriculture. Washington, D.C.: USDA.

Howe, F. W. 1911. Agricultural Education in Secondary Schools. Papers read at the Second Annual Meeting of the American Association for the Advancement of Science, Columbus, Ohio, November 14, 1911.

Moore, G. E. 1985. Where are you when we need you, Rufus W. Stimson? Paper presented at the National Agriculture Education Research Meeting, Atlanta, December 6, 1985.

Moore, G. E. 1987. The status of agricultural education prior to the Smith-Hughes Act. The Agricultural Education Magazine 59(February):8–10.

National Assessment for Educational Progress (NAEP). 1982. Graduates may lack tomorrow's basics. NAEP Newsletter 15:18.

National Commission on Excellence in Education. 1983. A Nation at Risk: The Imperative for Educational Reform. Washington, D.C.: U.S. Government Printing Office.

National FFA Organization. 1986. Participation in Selected FFA Activities. Alexandria, Va.: National FFA Organization.

National Research Council (NRC). 1985. Research Briefings 1985: Report of the Research Briefing Panel on Biotechnology in Agriculture. Reprint. Washington, D.C.: National Academy Press.

National Research Council (NRC). 1987a. Agricultural Biotechnology: Strategies for National Competitiveness. Washington, D.C.: National Academy Press.

National Research Council (NRC). 1987b. Regulating Pesticides in Food: The Delaney Paradox. Washington, D.C.: National Academy Press.

National Science Board (NSB) Commission on Precollege Education in Mathematics, Science, and Technology. 1983. Educating Americans for the 21st Century. CPCE-NSF-03. Washington, D.C.: NSF.

National Science Foundation (NSF) and U.S. Department of Education (USDE). 1980. Science and Engineering Education for the 1980s and Beyond. Washington, D.C.: NSF.

Office of Technology Assessment (OTA). 1986. Technology, Public Policy, and the Changing Structure of American Agriculture. OTA-F-285. Washington, D.C.: U.S. Government Printing Office.

Petrulis, M., B. L. Green, F. Hines, R. Nolan, and J. Sommer. 1987. How Is Farm Financial Stress Affecting Rural America? Agricultural Economic Report No. 568. Washington, D.C.: Economic Research Service, USDA.

P. L. #64-347 (39 STAT. 929; 20 U.S.C. Sec. 11–16 and 18–28.)

P. L. #98-524 (98 STAT. 2435; 20 U.S.C. 2301 et seq.)

P. L. #88-210 (77 STAT. 403 et seq.; 20 U.S.C. 1241 et seq.)

Rosenfeld, S. A. 1984. Vocational agriculture: A model for education reform. Education Week, September 26.

Snedden, D. 1918. Agricultural education—what is it? School and Society 7(January): 66–71.

Swanson, Gordon. Testimony before Committee on Agricultural Education in Secondary Schools, April 14, 1986. Chicago Board of Trade, Chicago, Ill.

Tenney, A. W. 1977. The FFA at 50—A Golden Past—A Brighter Future. Alexandria, Va.: FFA.

True, A. C. 1929. A History of Agricultural Education in the United States: 1785–1925. Washington, D.C.: U.S. Government Printing Office.

U.S. Department of Education (USDE). Economic Research Service. 1985. Economic Indicators of the Farm Sector: National Financial Summary, 1985. ECIFS5-2. Washington, D.C.: USDA.

U.S. Department of Education (USDE). 1984. The Nation Responds: Recent Efforts to Improve Education. Washington, D.C.: U.S. Government Printing Office.

U.S. Department of Commerce Bureau of the Census and USDA Economic Research Service. 1986. Farm population of the United States, 1985. P-27. 59:(July).

Warmbrod, J. R. 1962. State Policies for Distributing State and Federal Funds for Vocational Education in Agriculture to Local School Districts. Ph.D. dissertation. University of Illinois, Urbana.

Index